AQA Environm Science

GCSE

Kevin Byrne

with Clive Jones

Nelson Thornes

Published in 2009 by:
Nelson Thornes Ltd
Delta Place
27 Bath Road
CHELTENHAM
GL53 7TH
United Kingdom

09 10 11 12 13 / 10 9 8 7 6 5 4 3 2 1

A catalogue record for this book is available from the British
Library.

ISBN 978 1 4085 0396 6

Cover photograph by Alamy/Keith Morris

Illustrations include artwork drawn by Peters and Zabransky
and GreenGate Publishing

Page make-up by GreenGate Publishing, Tonbridge, Kent

Printed and bound in Spain by Graphycems

Contents

Nelson Thornes and AQA

Nelson Thornes has worked in partnership with AQA to make sure that this book offers you the best possible support for your GCSE course. All the content has been approved by the senior examining team at AQA, so you can be sure that it gives you just what you need when you are preparing for your exams.

How to use this book

This book covers everything you need for your course.

Learning Objectives

At the beginning of each section or topic you'll find a list of Learning Objectives based on the requirements of the specification, so you can make sure you are covering everything you need to know for the exam.

Objectives

First objective.

Second objective.

AQA Examiner's Tips

Don't forget to look at the AQA Examiner's Tips throughout the book to help you with your study and prepare for your exam.

AQA Examiner's tip

Don't forget to look at the AQA Examiner's Tips throughout the book to help you with your study and prepare for your exam.

AQA Examination-style Questions

These offer opportunities to practise doing questions in the style that you can expect in your exam so that you can be fully prepared on the day.

AQA examination questions are reproduced by permission of the Assessment and Qualifications Alliance.

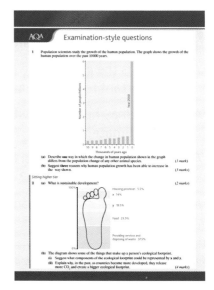

Visit **www.nelsonthornes.com/aqagcse** for more information.

This student book contains everything you need to know for the AQA Environmental Science GCSE, and also should help you to apply your knowledge to new situations when answering exam questions.

■ What is the GCSE Environmental Science course about?

During this GCSE course you will be looking at and learning about some of the big environmental issues that affect our lives today and in the future. This course is divided into two parts.

In part A you will look at *three contemporary issues* facing environmental scientists, and learn how these are central to the work they do.

In part B you will study *two environmental management issues* which will help you understand how scientists use their expertise and knowledge to protect and manage the natural resources around us.

Part A – The contemporary issues

The contemporary issues considered in this course are Population and sustainability, Energy resources and Global climate change.

A1 Population and sustainability

The global human population is growing at an ever-increasing rate. Environmental scientists are worried that the size of the population may outstrip the Earth's ability to support it. Chapter A1 covers four main questions that concern scientists when considering the problems caused by an increasing population. This chapter is divided into four sections:

- A1.1 Why is the human population increasing so fast?
- A1.2 Are some lifestyles more sustainable than others?
- A1.3 How may food supplies be increased to provide for the growing population?
- A1.4 Are the developments in world food production sustainable?

A2 Energy resources

Environmental scientists believe that, in the future, global energy consumption will increase significantly due to population growth and increasing living standards. Chapter A2 covers the main questions facing scientists when considering the problems of energy conservation and alternative energy supplies. This chapter is divided into four sections:

- A2.1 How are energy resources used?
- A2.2 How can energy consumption be reduced?
- A2.3 Why is the continued use of fossil fuels unsustainable?
- A2.4 What alternative energy technologies are available?

A3 Global climate change

Most scientists who study the atmosphere now believe the amount of greenhouse gases is leading to significant changes in the Earth's climate, with the potential to cause harm to natural ecosystems and serious problems for people in many parts of the world. Chapter A3 covers the main questions that scientists try to answer when considering measures to deal with global climate change. This chapter is divided into four sections:

- A3.1 Why is the greenhouse effect important for life on Earth?
- A3.2 How may human activities change the climate?
- A3.3 What are the potential effects of global climate change?
- A3.4 Can global climate change be stopped?

Part B – The environmental management issues

The environmental management issues that you will study are about the management of wildlife resources and the management of water resources. You will learn how environmental scientists use their expertise and knowledge of environmental issues to protect and manage the natural resources around us.

B1 The management of wildlife resources

Environmental scientists identify species that are in danger and the threats to them. They also develop management strategies to manage and conserve wildlife habitats and species. Chapter B1 considers three questions that concern environmental scientists when managing particular wildlife habitats This chapter is divided into three sections:

- B1.1 Why is there a need to manage wildlife?
- B1.2 How is wildlife conserved?
- B1.3 Can the wild food sources of the oceans be exploited sustainably?

B2 The management of water resources

The Environment Agency is the UK government organisation looking after the environment, managing water resources and working to prevent floods and control water pollution. Environmental scientists are employed by water companies to assist in the management of the public supply, and water and sewage treatment. Chapter B2 considers some of the questions that concern those that manage our water supply companies. This chapter is divided into three sections:

- B2.1 How is water allocated to different uses in the UK?
- B2.2 Where do supplies of drinking water come from and how are they treated to make them safe?
- B2.3 What happens to waste water?

And finally…

Environmental Science is a practical, hands-on science so as well as learning about the topics through reading, writing and listening, you will be given the opportunity to investigate issues using your scientific knowledge and skills in practical activities.

You will be assessed through a written examination and practical investigation work:

- **Examination**

  Foundation or Higher Tier

  Written paper – 2 hours

  120 marks = 75%

  10–16 compulsory questions (short answer, structured and longer answer).

- **Investigations**
  (1) **Investigative Skills Assignment (ISA)**

  Externally set, internally assessed test – 45 minutes

  34 marks

  (2) **Practical Skills Assessment (PSA)**

  Continual assessment during practical work

  6 marks

  Total – 40 marks = 25%

This book has been written to support you in developing the knowledge and skills you will need to succeed in both the examination and your investigation work.

■ Special features of this book

Environmental Scientists@Work

Environmental Scientists@Work boxes explain how environmental scientists in a variety of occupations apply their knowledge and understanding of the current topic to tackle environmental issues. This information will highlight how environmental science impacts on every aspect of our everyday lives and what career paths might be available to you as a result of studying the subject.

How Science Works

The How Science Works section (pages 7–15) and activities within How Science Works boxes throughout this book will encourage you to think like a scientist and develop the skills and knowledge needed to carry out your Investigative Skills Assignment (ISA) and other practical work successfully.

Sitting higher tier

Find out whether or not you will be taking the Foundation or Higher Tier exam. If you are taking Higher Tier, you will need to study and digest the extra material contained in the Higher Tier sections.

Key terms

Specialist terms or really important terms have been identified as key terms. They are highlighted in blue type where they first appear in the text, and an explanation for each term is given in the Key Terms box as well as in the Glossary on page 137. It is important for the exam and your investigation work to learn what each term means and when to use it.

How Science Works

Environmental scientists, like all other scientists, are trained in scientific method. This involves making predictions and gathering and using evidence. These are important skills that you need to develop throughout your course. The ideas in 'How Science Works' will be tested in your controlled assessments and in the written exam papers.

■ What you already know

Here is a quick reminder of what you should know about 'How Science Works' from your Key Stage 3 Science. You will find this knowledge useful as you work through this chapter and will build on it throughout your GCSE course.

- You've already done lots of practical work and know that it is important to keep yourself and others safe.
- At the start of an investigation, you make a prediction which you can test.
- You make a plan which describes what you are going to change and what you are going to measure and record.
- You think about factors that need to be controlled.
- You think about doing repeats of the investigation to get more data.
- During your practical work, you record your observations, usually in a table.
- You then present your data in the most suitable way, which might be a graph or bar chart.
- You make conclusions to explain your results.
- Finally, you think about ways of improving what you did.

■ We all use science all of the time!

Think about when you first picked up the TV's remote control, your MP3 player or mobile phone. How did you work out what buttons did what? You probably played around with it. You knew that pressing buttons would change things on the screen (you had **knowledge**). You pressed buttons and watched what happened (you made **observations**). You guessed what pressing a particular button would do (you made a **prediction**) and then pressed it (**experimented**). In other words, you went into scientist mode!

You established **facts** about what the buttons did. Eventually, by pressing a particular button lots of times and ensuring that it always achieved the same thing, you knew that your results were **reliable**.

In this chapter you will learn:

about scientific method

about different types of variables

the difference between accuracy and precision

how to present data

how to interpret data

about ethical issues in scientific investigations.

Key terms

Reliable: data is reliable if someone else can repeat what you did and get the same results.

Activity

Rohit and Melissa investigated which material was the best insulator. Rohit thought that foam would be the best because his dad had wrapped foam around their hot water tank. Melissa thought cotton wool would be best because it traps a lot of air. They heated 1 litre of water to 60 °C. They poured 200 cm³ of this water into each of five flasks. Each flask had been covered with a different insulating material (see Diagram **A**). They recorded the temperature of the water in each flask every 15 minutes for one hour. They recorded their results in a table and then drew a graph.

1 a   What was Melissa's prediction?

   b   What was the variable they chose to change? (We call it the **independent variable**.)

   c   What was the variable measured to judge the effect of varying the independent variable? (We call it the **dependent variable** because its value depends on the independent variable.)

   d   Write down one variable that they controlled.

   e   Write down one variable that they did not control.

   f   Identify one source of error in their method.

   g   Draw a table that they could use to record their results.

   h   On a graph of their results, what label would go on the horizontal (x) axis?

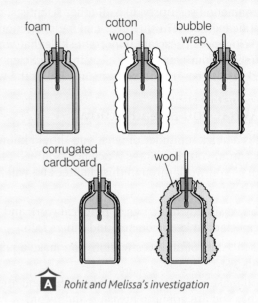

A *Rohit and Melissa's investigation*

■ Starting an investigation

What to measure

You already know about **dependent variables** and **independent variables**. These can be split into four types:

- Categoric variable – one that is based on non-numerical data, e.g. colour of eye.
- Discrete variable – one that is described in whole numbers, e.g. number of leaves on a dandelion plant.
- Ordered variable – one where the data can be put into order but not given an actual number, e.g. leaves growing in bright sunlight are bigger than those growing in the shade.
- Continuous variable – one that is measured and that can have an infinite number of values, e.g. length of a leaf.

When designing your investigation, you should try to make sure that you are measuring a continuous variable. If that is impossible, try to use ordered data.

Reliability and validity

When you are designing your investigation you should remember that another student should be able to repeat your investigation and get the same result. If they can, your result is **reliable**. For your investigation to be **valid**, you must also ensure that your results enable you to answer the original question.

Good science often begins with good observation skills.

Key terms

Independent variable: the variable that you, as investigator, change or select.

Dependent variable: the variable that you are measuring each time you change the independent variable.

Validity: the extent to which your results answer the question asked. Valid data has to be reliable and relevant.

Hypothesis: an idea that might explain the relationship under investigation.

Fair test: one in which the only thing affecting the dependent variable is the independent variable that you are changing or selecting.

Activity

John's dad has observed that his green beans are growing much better at the top of his allotment than at the bottom. He asks John to investigate and tells him that if he can come up with a reasonable explanation, he can have the latest computer game.

John goes to the allotment. He sees that the plants at the top are taller and have more beans than the plants at the bottom. The bottom has more weeds too (see Diagram **B**).

He knows that plants need sunlight, water and soil nutrients to grow well. He looks around the allotment. There are no tall trees casting shade. There is no obvious reason why the plants at the top and bottom are getting different amounts of sunlight. John looks at the other plants growing in the allotment. There are more small weeds growing at the bottom than at the top. This gives him an idea. It may be, he thinks, that the weeds are taking nutrients and water out of the soil and this is why the beans are not growing as well there.

John has combined good observation skills with his knowledge of how plants compete and grow to come up with a great idea – a **hypothesis** – to explain the growth of his dad's bean plants. Next, he makes a prediction. 'If I pull out all of the weeds at the bottom, the bean plants will grow taller and will carry more beans'. Now he is ready to test his prediction.

Observation + knowledge $\longrightarrow$ hypothesis $\longrightarrow$ prediction $\longrightarrow$ investigation

He pulls out all the weeds. Within weeks, the bean plants at the bottom are growing just as well as those at the top of the allotment.

John has predicted that there will be a relationship between variables:

Independent variable: Number of weed plants growing around the beans

Dependent variable: Growth of beans (which can be measured as number or mass or length).

All other variables were control variables which needed to be kept constant to make it a **fair test**.

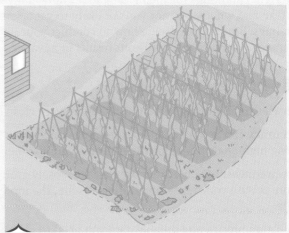

B *John's dad's allotment*

2 Can you think of a control variable in John's investigation?

To make it a fair test, John could not do anything else to either part of the allotment. He could not for example, add more fertiliser to the beans at the bottom because then he would not know if improved growth was due to his weeding or his adding fertiliser. In a fair test, only the one chosen independent variable is allowed to influence the dependent variable.

Activity

Amy investigated how much water people in her village used. Her hypothesis was that households that had water meters would use less water than those that did not have a meter.

3 Which data should she have collected to test this hypothesis?

a The cost of an average water meter.

b Average water use in houses with single people and with families.

c The time when water use was greatest.

d Average water use in houses with and without meters.

C *A household water meter*

Choosing values of a variable

Look back at the Activities on page 8. Before Rohit and Melissa started their actual investigation into which material was the best insulator, they did a quick trial run. They filled the flasks with the warm water and took temperature readings every 5 minutes. But they soon realized that this wasn't long enough for the temperature to change much. This is how they knew to make recordings every 15 minutes in the real investigation.

Trial runs are useful because they help you work out whether you have the right conditions for the investigation, how many readings you need to take and whether or not you are likely to get a sensible range of readings. So, you can decide how to conduct your investigation and prepare your table to record your results in advance.

Accuracy and precision

Accurate measurements are those that are very close to the real value.

Accuracy can be improved by carefully taking repeat measurements, using high-quality equipment and being careful when taking readings.

Precise measurements are those that are closely grouped together. The more precise your repeat measurements are, the more reliable your data.

To obtain precise and reliable data you need to repeat your tests as often as necessary and ensure that you carry out the tests in exactly the same way each time. But be careful, just because your results are precise, it does not mean that they are accurate!

Taking measurements

When you are taking measurements and recording your data in a table, keep a constant lookout for **anomalies**. Anomalies are measurements or results that are clearly out of line. If you spot one, repeat the measurement to see if you made an error the first time. Check that the pattern you are getting as you change the independent variable is what you expected. If it is not, then you may need to check for other anomalies or consider another hypothesis. If you find an anomaly after you have finished collecting your data, do not use it when working out your results but try to think of a reason for it.

The difference between accurate and precise results

Imagine measuring the temperature after a set time when a fuel is used to heat a fixed volume of water. Two students repeated this experiment, four times each. Their results are marked on the thermometer scales in Diagram **D**:

- A precise set of repeat readings will be grouped closely together.
- An accurate set of readings will have a mean (average) close to the true value.

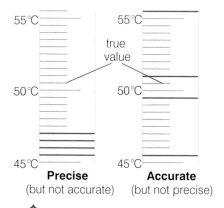

Precise
(but not accurate)

Accurate
(but not precise)

true value

D *Precise and accurate measurements*

Presenting your data

Tables are a good way of recording and presenting your data. Always draw your table before you begin any actual practical work. This helps you to be clear about what you are actually going to measure or count. Your table should have a title, labels and units.

Sometimes you will have recorded a lot of data and it will be impossible to get a clear picture of what is going on just by looking at it in its raw form.

> **AQA** *Examiner's tip*
>
> Make sure you know the difference between accuracy and precision!

Activity

Sophie investigated whether pollution from vehicles was affecting the growth of lichen on gravestones. She had predicted that the amount of lichen on gravestones would increase the further away the stones were from the road.

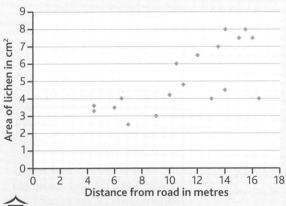

E *Lichen growing on gravestones*

Sophie's recordings are shown in Table **G**.

4 **a** Looking quickly at the data in Table **G**, can you spot any clear pattern?

Just looking at the figures in the table, it is not easy to get a clear picture. But if we plot the data in a graph…

F *Sophie's data presented in a graph*

… things become much clearer!

b Describe the pattern you can see in Graph **F** of Sophie's data of lichen on gravestones and distance from the polluting road. Is there a pattern (trend) in the graph which shows lichen cover with distance from the road?

G	Sophie's data	
Stone number	Distance from road/m	Area of lichen/cm²
1	4.5	3.6
2	4.5	3.3
3	6.0	3.5
4	7.0	2.5
5	6.5	4.0
6	9.0	3.0
7	11.0	4.8
8	10.0	4.2
9	12.0	6.5
10	10.5	6.0
11	15.0	7.5
12	14.0	8.0
13	13.5	7.0
14	15.0	7.5
15	16.5	4.0
16	15.5	8.0
17	16.0	7.5
18	15.5	8.0
19	13.0	4.0
20	14.0	4.5

Bar charts

Use a bar chart when you have a categoric or ordered independent variable and a continuous dependent variable, for example, numbers of different tree species in two woodlands (see Table **H** and Bar Chart **I**).

Line graphs

Use a line graph when both your independent and dependent variables are continuous, for example, height of plants grown at different temperatures (see Table **J** and Graph **K**).

J *Heights of plants grown at different temperatures*

Temperature/°C	Mean height of seedlings at day 14/mm
5	6
10	8
15	12
20	18
25	24

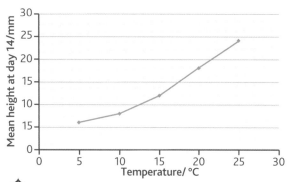

K *Effect of temperature on height of seedlings*

H *Number of trees*

Woodland A		Woodland B	
Ash	26	Oak	20
Birch	10	Hazel	6
Holly	2	Ash	3

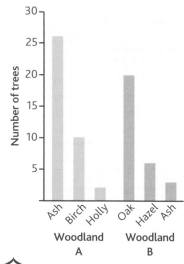

I *Tree species in two woodlands*

■ Science doesn't prove anything

Graph **K** provides evidence that increasing the temperature over the range shown leads to taller seedlings but it does not *prove* it. Other variables may be responsible. Scientists do not prove anything. Rather, they gather more and more evidence and control as many variables as possible so that they can be as sure as they can be about the relationship they are investigating.

Scientists publish their investigations in journals which are read by thousands of other scientists all around the world. They critically analyse each other's investigations and repeat others' investigations to try and ensure that the published results are reliable.

Politicians and planners then use the best available scientific data to make what are often difficult decisions. For example, the UK government has to plan where the country is going to get its energy from in future decades. This involves analysing a huge amount of information from different sources.

But even with reliable data, making decisions like these is not easy, not least because it is often possible to draw opposite conclusions from any set of data! The following activity illustrates this.

How much should we spend on energy-saving measures?

Which countries can we import coal from?

How much do we have to reduce CO_2 emissions by?

How long will North Sea oil and gas last?

Should we develop new nuclear power stations?

Can renewables make us self-sufficient in energy?

L *Politicians must use scientific data to make difficult decisions*

Activities

Carbon dioxide is the most important greenhouse gas. Table **M** shows changes in the amounts of carbon dioxide emitted from different sources in the United Kingdom (UK) between 1990 and 2006. The UK government has set a target of cutting UK carbon dioxide emissions by 20 per cent by 2010, based on the amount emitted in 1990.

M *Carbon dioxide emissions in the UK*

	1990	1995	2000	2005	2006
Transport	109	111	116	120	120
Energy supply	242	208	200	218	221
Business	109	104	104	93	92
Residential	80	81	87	85	81
Other	49	45	42	42	42
Total	590	549	549	557	557

5 Imagine that you are a politician who believes that the UK government is making progress towards meeting its carbon dioxide reduction target. Identify two pieces of evidence from Table **M** which you could use to support this view.

6 Now, imagine that you are an environmental campaigner who believes that the UK government is unlikely to meet its carbon dioxide reduction target. How could you use evidence from the table to support this view?

Source: AQA, 2009

Presenting results in tables and graphs helps us to decide if there is a link between the variables we have investigated. The links between variables may be due to chance, due to association or they may be causal. You must weigh up all the evidence to decide which is most likely.

Activity

Graph **N** shows how levels of carbon dioxide in the atmosphere have changed over the past 1000 years.

Graph **O** shows how the average global temperature has changed from 1860 to 2003.

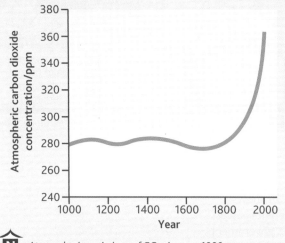

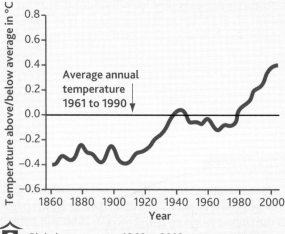

N *Atmospheric emissions of CO_2 since AD 1000*   **O** *Global temperature, 1860 to 2003*

Many scientists believe that global temperature has increased because carbon dioxide concentrations have increased. That is, they believe that there is a causal relationship between the two variables.

7 Look at the two graphs. Which of the following statements are correct conclusions from the data?

a Overall, between 1860 and 2003, average global temperature has increased

b Between 1000 and 1700, the level of carbon dioxide in the atmosphere remained steady

c Since 1700, the level of carbon dioxide has increased

d Increasing global temperature has caused an increase in carbon dioxide levels

e Increasing carbon dioxide levels have caused average global temperature to increase

Did you realise that **a–c** are correct conclusions but that the graphs do not support conclusions **d** or **e**? Even though, using other evidence, many scientists believe that increasing CO_2 levels have contributed to increasing temperatures, this data do not show causality.

◼ Ethical issues

Whenever we carry out an experiment or investigation, we need to think about what effect we might have on other organisms or the environment. For example, we may be concerned that a new pesticide may harm useful insects such as bees. In order to test this, is it ever acceptable to treat some bees with the pesticide? In other words, is it acceptable to harm a few insects in an effort to protect the rest of the population?

Article **P** gives details about the Republic of Kiribati.

Pacific Islanders' Climate Change Fear

- The Republic of Kiribati is a country in the Pacific Ocean. It is made up of about 30 small islands.

- Almost all the land in Kiribati is less than two metres above sea level.

- There are very few motor vehicles and no large factories or power stations on the islands.

- The people of Kiribati are worried that an increase in the greenhouse effect will cause the sea level to rise so that their islands are flooded.

- Many of the islanders say that climate change will not be their fault and that people in more economically developed countries (MEDCs) should be doing more to reduce the amount of carbon dioxide they emit.

8 a If you lived in Kiribati, what types of energy would you want the governments of MEDCs to choose over the next 30 years?

   b What **ten** things would you encourage individuals living in an MEDC to do to reduce their carbon footprint?

Source: AQA, 2009

Summary

Observation is often a good starting point for an investigation.

Hypotheses are 'good ideas' that help to predict and design an investigation.

Careful use of the correct equipment, with repeat measurements will improve accuracy and reliability.

Anomalous results are those that are out of line with the rest of the results. These measurements should be repeated, or discarded if the data collection is complete.

Science does not aim to prove things. Rather, it builds up evidence to support an explanation.

Scientists consider ethical issues when they are designing investigations.

Refer back to this section whenever you need help with a How Science Works activity in later chapters and when you conduct your Investigative Skills Assignment (ISA).

A1 Population and sustainability

A1.1 Why is the human population increasing so fast?

In 2008, the global human population reached 6.7 billion. Population scientists have predicted that it will increase to over 9 billion by 2050. Such predictions are important because government scientists across the world need to plan how we are going to provide enough food, water and essential services for these extra people.

Environmental scientists@work

Planning for India's water supply in 2050

India has the second highest population in the world – and it is growing quickly. Since 1997, Professor Saifuddin Soz has been the Water Resources Minister. It is his job to ensure that, by 2050, when the population is predicted to stabilise, there is sufficient water for everyone in India. Water scientists (hydrologists) working for the Indian government have identified many problems that will increase the demand on a diminishing clean water supply and must find solutions.

Professor Soz has written to the ministers for housing, agriculture and population to ask for a coordinated approach to water resource planning. Predicting the population of each state in 2050 is just the first step. Hydrologists must now try to estimate how climate change will affect rainfall and evaporation so that they can estimate how much water will be available in each state. Once that is done, decisions can be taken on where to build new reservoirs and where underground supplies need to be protected, and so on. At the same time, the Housing Minister must plan for the number of new houses that will be needed in each city, if the continuing growth of slums is to be avoided.

Source: www.indiawaterportal.org

In this section you will learn:

- about trends in human population growth
- about the difference in population growth rates of MEDCs and LEDCs
- how science and technology have affected population growth
- why the population growth rate of some countries is slowing down.

What are the trends in human population growth?

The Earth is about 4.5 billion years old. If we condense all of that time into a single day, then dinosaurs arrived just before 11 pm and humans appeared for the first time just a few seconds before midnight. But what an impact we've had in those few seconds!

- Until about 1800, the human population grew slowly.
- The population didn't reach 1 billion until around 1830.
- It took another 100 years for it to reach 2 billion.
- But by 1960, just 30 years later, it had already grown to 3 billion.
- The next billion people took just 15 years, and just 12 years later (1987) it had become 5 billion.
- Now, our planet supports 6.7 billion people and this increases by 2.4 people every second or around 207 000 every day! (Look at Diagram **A**.)

Key terms

Birth rate: the ratio of live births in an area to the population of that area, usually expressed as 'per thousand (people) per year'.

Death rate: the ratio of deaths in an area to the population of that area, usually expressed as 'per thousand (people) per year'.

Population growth rate: a measure of population change, usually the natural rate of increase of the population. Birth rate ± death rate (per year).

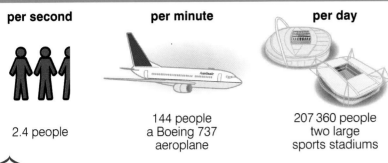

per second

2.4 people

per minute

144 people
a Boeing 737
aeroplane

per day

207 360 people
two large
sports stadiums

A *The human population is increasing so quickly that enough people are born each day to fill two Olympic stadiums!*

Over the past 200 years, there has been a human population explosion (see Bar chart **B**). When the populations of other species increase rapidly like this, it usually ends in disaster. Food supplies may run out and many animals starve or disease may kill a huge proportion of the population. Scientists have developed agricultural systems that aim to produce enough food for everyone on the planet (Section A1.3) and, by providing clean water supplies and modern medicines, have prevented or cured many killer diseases. Section A1.4 will look at why, if there is enough food to go round, millions of people are still starving.

However, what Diagram **B** does not show us is that, in recent years, the **rate of population growth** has slowed down – in other words, although the population is still increasing, it is not increasing anywhere near as quickly as it did in the 20th century. This is because in most **MEDCs** (More Economically Developed Countries), **birth rates** are falling and the population is becoming stable. However, in almost all Less Economically Developed Countries (**LEDCs**), birth rates are high and rising and so too is their population as **death rates** may fall (see Graph **C**).

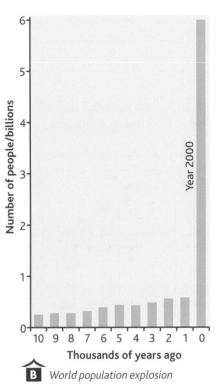

B *World population explosion*

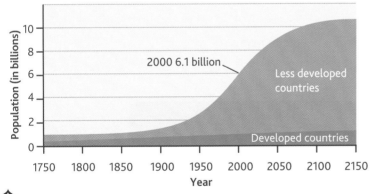

2000 6.1 billion

Less developed countries

Developed countries

C *Population changes in developed countries and less developed countries*
Source: © 2001 Population Reference Bureau

LEDCs tend to have high existing populations and high birth rates, so most population growth is expected to occur in these regions (see Table **D** and Graph **E** on the next page).

D *Increase in population between 2000 and 2015*

Region	Population increase (millions)
South Asia	352.0
East Asia and Pacific	229.7
Sub-Saharan Africa	178.5
Latin America and Caribbean	98.1
Middle East and North Africa	84.8
High income	72.2

Source: World Bank estimates

By 2075, it is expected that 90 per cent of the world's population will live in developing countries.

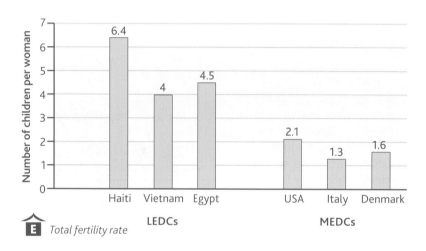

E *Total fertility rate*

So, we need to ask ourselves the question: Why do people in many LEDCs have large families?

More children means more help fetching water and fuel wood.

Children provide care for elderly parents.

Being able to produce many children may be seen as a status symbol or indication of virility.

Lack of access to, or unwillingness to use contraception.

F *Why do people in many LEDCs have large families?*

Activities

1 Copy and complete the following paragraph using the words provided.

appetite   MEDCs   increased   population   decreased

women   LEDCs   hungry people   poverty

The human .... has .... rapidly since 1800. The time taken for the population to increase by another billion has .... The population of .... is stable or falling. The population of .... is increasing rapidly. This means, that by 2050, most of the world's population will live in ....

2 What type of variable is total fertility rate (see page 22)?

a Categoric

b Discrete

c Ordered

d Continuous

How have science and technology affected population growth?

The huge increase in human population since 1800 is due to various factors:

- **Improved sanitation – toilets, drains and sewage treatment works.** In the past, many people died from diseases such as cholera and dysentery, spread via water or food that was contaminated by faeces.

- **The provision of clean water supplies.** For example, before water engineers began to filter and chemically treat drinking water, cholera was responsible for hundreds of thousands of deaths in several pandemics. In Europe, diarrhoeal diseases are responsible for just 0.01 deaths per 1000 people. By contrast, in South–East Asia, the figure is 0.36 deaths per 1000 people per year.

- **Massive increases in food production.** The use of machinery (mechanisation), fertilisers, pesticides and improved varieties and animal breeds has meant that, within MEDCs, there is plenty of food for everybody and supermarkets stock over 25 000 different types of food. In LEDCs, people eat much the same thing every day. In Nepal, for example, the daily diet of an ordinary family is dhal bat (rice and lentils).

- **Improved scientific understanding of the causes and treatment of disease.** Medical scientists have identified which organisms are potential pathogens (capable of causing disease). Water engineers and food scientists have developed the means of avoiding disease. Advances in medical science means that many diseases can be treated. An example is given on the next page.

Taking water for granted

Living in the UK, it is very easy to take basic facilities such as clean water and flushing toilets for granted. The population of the UK is about 61 million. Nearly every person in the UK has access to clean drinking water and a flushing toilet.

The population of India is about 1.2 billion – that's 19 times greater than the UK! Two-thirds of the population have inadequate sanitation. In other words, in India, around 700 million men, women and children have no toilets or sewers or ways of treating their waste. They have to defecate in the bushes by the side of the road or into the streams and rivers that other people drink from or bathe in…

Tuberculosis (TB) is caused by a species of bacteria that enters the body when infected droplets from coughing or sneezing are breathed in (one good reason for using a tissue!). Worldwide, it is a major killer – in 2005, 1.6 million people died from TB. It does not discriminate – Keats, Chopin, Edgar Allan Poe, Robert Louis Stevenson, Franz Kafka, King Tutankhamen and George Orwell all suffered from tuberculosis!

Scientists have studied TB in great detail. They understand how it gets into our bodies, the effects it has and how to treat it. Graph **G** shows information about the number of reported cases of tuberculosis in the UK during the period 1920 to 1990.

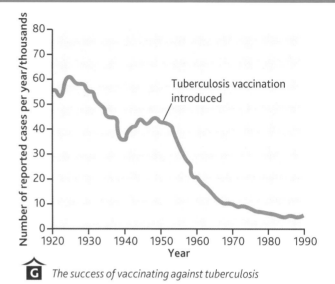

G *The success of vaccinating against tuberculosis*

Activity

3 Study Table **H** which gives information about the four countries shown on Map **I**.

H

	Country			
	A	**B**	**C**	**D**
Population growth rate/per thousand per year	5.8	22.2	15.8	0.6
Birth rate/No. of births per 1000 people per year	12.5	34.6	22.2	10.6
Death rate/No. of deaths per 1000 people per year	6.7	12.4	6.4	10.0
Infant mortality rate/No. of deaths per 1000 births per year	4.8	64.6	32.3	4.9
Age structure				
% 0–14 yrs	18.8	41.1	31.5	16.9
% 64+ yrs	13.3	3.2	5.2	16.0
Life expectancy/years	81.5	53.3	69.2	78.8
Literacy rate/% of population able to read and write	99	68	61	99
Electricity consumption/billion kWh	259.8	3.4	488.5	348

Source: Adapted from the CIA World Factbook

a From Table **H**, identify the country that appears to have a surprisingly high:
   i literacy rate
   ii death rate
b The countries shown are the UK, Cameroon, Australia and India. But can you work out which country is which?

If you have access to the internet search for 'CIA World Factbook'.

For each country you will be able to access lots of fascinating data. Make your own comparison table using some of the other sorts of data. For example, you could make a table showing the three richest and poorest countries in Africa and see if there is a relationship between wealth and the number of people suffering from AIDS.

I *Location map*

How science works

Estimating adult literacy rates in Africa

Imagine that you are a population scientist. You would know from previous research that if you want to control population growth, you need to increase female literacy rates. In other words, teaching teenage girls to read and write is the most effective form of contraception because it gives them aspirations beyond becoming mothers at an early age.

It's your job to estimate adult literacy rates for two countries in Africa. Which of the following would be sensible things to do to ensure that your estimates were fair and reliable?

(Remember: the literacy rate = the proportion of people in a country that can read and write at the age of 15 years.)

A   Test every single person in both countries to see if they can read and write

B   Test equal numbers of males and females in each country

C   Test an equal proportion of male and female 15 year olds in each country

D   Test 10 boys and girls, all aged 15, in each country and then multiply up

E   Record the number of comics sold to 15 year olds in each country

The answer is just C. It would be impossibly expensive and time-consuming to test every single person. In any case, only 15 year olds need to be measured. Nor is it very sensible to measure equal numbers of males and females in each country without knowing what the total population of each country is. If the population of one country is 5 times greater than the other, then we need to test 5 times more people there. Testing just 10 people in each country is too small a sample. Few African countries sell comics to children – there are more urgent things to spend money on – and in any case, this does not really tell us anything about literacy rates.

When doing real science, we need to ensure that we are testing fairly (in this case, an equal proportion of males and females) and that our sample size is adequate.

J *Adult literacy in Africa*

Why is the population growth rate of some countries slowing down?

Population scientists predict that the populations of many MEDCs, especially those in Europe, will shrink over the next 50 years. Birth rates are falling and, in most EU countries, the **total fertility rate** is less than 2.

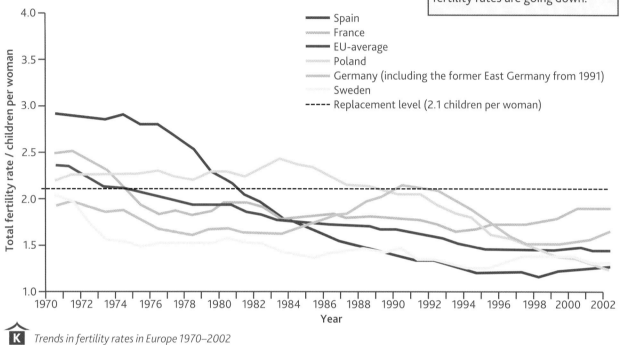

K *Trends in fertility rates in Europe 1970–2002*

Source: Council of Europe, www.coe.int

There are several reasons for this:

1 Children are no longer seen as being essential contributors to a family's income. At the same time, the cost of feeding, clothing and educating children is increasing. So there is an economic argument against having many (or any!) children.

2 In the past, many children died during birth or early childhood and couples safeguarded against this by having big families. Improved maternity and post-natal care and all-round better medical provision means that this is no longer the case. Similarly, men and women now have easy access to reliable methods of birth control and can effectively decide exactly how many children they rear.

3 The nature of society has also changed and has contributed to falling birth rates. In the past, many women were expected only to become housewives and not go to university or embark upon careers. This has changed dramatically. Now, there are equal numbers of young men and women entering university and an increasing proportion of women choose careers rather than child-bearing, or they have children later than their parents and grandparents would have done.

Key terms

Total fertility rate: the average number of children each woman has over her lifetime.

4 The rise of the 'consumer society' may also have contributed to declining populations in MEDCs. When considering the choice between having a second child or stopping at one child and being able to afford a new car every three years or exotic holidays, more and more people are choosing the latter!

5 Finally, there is much greater social acceptance of gay/lesbian relationships and these couples are less likely to have families.

Activities

4 Look at Graph **K** (the fertility graph).

a What was the first year in which the EU-average number of children per woman fell below 2?

b Why is 2.1 children sometimes called the replacement level?

5 Copy and complete the table, which compares population trends in MEDCs and LEDCs. Some answers have been written in to help you.

Characteristic	MEDC	LEDC
Birth rate		
Death rate		High
Population trend	Stable or decreasing	
Average number of children per woman		
Access to clean drinking water	High	
Access to adequate sanitation		

Summary

World population has grown very rapidly since 1800 and is expected to continue to increase.

Population scientists need to predict future populations so that governments can plan how to provide them with enough food and clean water.

Human population growth has been caused by improved food production, better sanitation and huge improvements in medical care.

Most of the expected population increase will be in LEDCs.

Birth rates in many MEDCs are falling and their populations are stable. There are medical, economic and social reasons for this trend.

A1.2 Are some lifestyles more sustainable than others?

Humans are having a huge, harmful impact on the planet and the population is increasing rapidly.

The global challenge is to work out how development can be made harmless (or less harmful) to the planet. Environmental scientists are employed by governments and environmental campaign groups to advise on **sustainable development**.

Heating Shropshire homes with leftovers

Greenfinch is an engineering firm in Ludlow, Shropshire. Working with the district council, their waste engineers have come up with a new way of making money and electricity out of all the waste food that people in Shropshire throw away.

Each household has been given a blue bin into which they put compostable bags filled with their food wastes. These are collected every week and taken to Greenfinch's anaerobic digester that breaks down the wastes into compost and biogas. The compost is sold to local allotment holders and gardeners and the biogas is burned to generate electricity that retailer, Marks and Spencer, has agreed to buy.

A An anaerobic digester

In this section you will learn:

what we mean by 'sustainable development'

about the demands that growing populations make on resources and the reasons why this may be unsustainable

why it is difficult to predict population growth

what we mean by 'ecological footprint'

about the ways in which we can make our lifestyles more sustainable.

Key terms

Sustainable: capable of being carried on forever, which means living within environmental limits.

Sustainable development: development which meets present needs without compromising the ability of future generations to achieve their needs and aspirations.

■ What is sustainable development?

Sustainable development is not an easy thing to define!

Activity

1 Working in groups of four:

a Score each statement in the box on the right according to how best you think it describes sustainable development. For example, if you think that A is the best definition, give it a score of 5. The worst definition gets a score of 1.

b When you have finished, compare your scores with the other groups in the class. Did one definition prove the overall winner?

Most scientists think that all of these have something to do with sustainable development. It involves using our natural resources wisely to meet people's needs but also ensuring that the world that we leave our children is at least as healthy as that we inherited from our parents.

Possible definitions of sustainable development

A Immediate preservation of all animals and plants so that no more species become extinct.

B Preserving and protecting all the different sorts of ecosystems like tropical rainforests, deserts and oceans in the world.

C Making sure that poor farmers in the Caribbean get a fair price from the big supermarkets for their bananas.

D Protecting natural resources like the soil, plants and animals whilst still using them as food and raw materials.

E The introduction of laws banning people from eating meat or driving 4×4s in cities.

The government believe that sustainable development means trying to achieve three things at once – a fair or just society, a healthy environment and a thriving economy.

B *Sustainable development: a fair society, a healthy environment and a thriving economy*

The National Forest

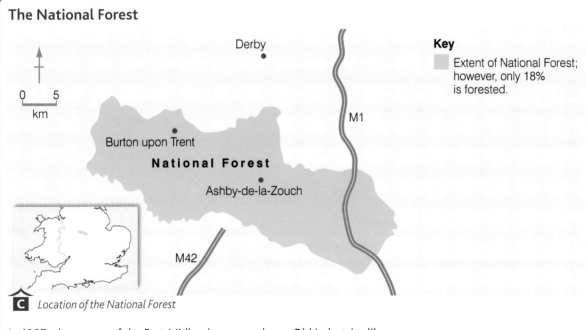

Key

▨ Extent of National Forest; however, only 18% is forested.

C *Location of the National Forest*

In 1987 a large area of the East Midlands was rundown. Old industries like mining had closed down. There were few jobs for young people. Many towns had boarded-up shops and derelict areas.

Since then, the National Forest Company's team of foresters, land use managers and ecologists have worked with local people, businesses, schools and wildlife charities to plant 7 million trees over a 200 square mile area. The landscape has been transformed, an annual wood fair attracts over 3000 people and hundreds of jobs in forestry, local cafes, B&Bs, garages, for example, have been created. The area has changed from somewhere you drive through to somewhere you drive to!

Environmental scientists@work

Activity

2   How is the National Forest helping to achieve:

■ a just society

■ a healthy environment

■ a thriving economy?

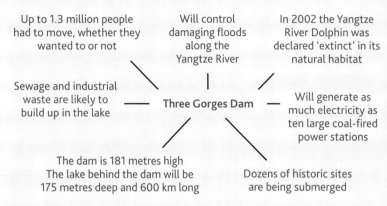

Activity

Diagram **D** gives details about the Three Gorges Dam in China.

Three Gorges Dam – disaster or sustainable development?

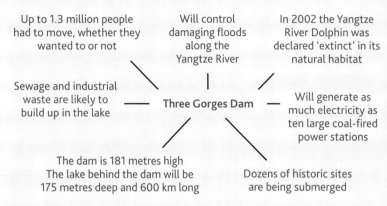

Up to 1.3 million people had to move, whether they wanted to or not

Will control damaging floods along the Yangtze River

In 2002 the Yangtze River Dolphin was declared 'extinct' in its natural habitat

Sewage and industrial waste are likely to build up in the lake

Three Gorges Dam

Will generate as much electricity as ten large coal-fired power stations

The dam is 181 metres high The lake behind the dam will be 175 metres deep and 600 km long

Dozens of historic sites are being submerged

D

Some people believe that the Three Gorges Dam is an example of sustainable development. Other people believe that it is a disaster and an example of unsustainable development.

3 Use the information in Diagram **D** and from books or the internet to make a table listing the arguments on both sides.

'The Three Gorges dam is sustainable development!'	'The Three Gorges dam isn't sustainable development!'
Hydroelectricity doesn't release carbon dioxide	Building the dam released huge amounts of carbon dioxide
Less coal mining will be needed	

What resources do people need?

As a population grows it demands more resources. One problem is that many of these resources are finite – once they are gone, they are gone!

First though, what is the difference between what people want and what they actually need?

Activity

4 Sort the list of needs into three boxes labelled 'Absolute basic need for my lifestyle', 'Nice, but not essential in my life' and 'Luxury goods and services'. Once you've done this, compare your lists with a friend!

Mobile phone	MP3 player	Education
Designer trainers	Heating	Free speech
Fridge	Paper	Umbrella
Holiday abroad	Football	Computer
A bath	Designer clothing	
A house	Bread	

Our basic needs are for water, food and shelter. Without these, we would die. Once we have these, we strive for things which we don't necessarily need, but which we want – education, healthcare, energy, clothing, furniture and appliances. These improve our standard of living. Then, to protect our quality of life, we demand attractive living spaces, unspoiled landscapes and recreational areas.

A family in Kent regard a fridge as a basic need. A family in Darfur, Sudan would regard it as a luxury. But we can be fairly sure that as countries develop, demand for water, food, energy, houses and appliances increases.

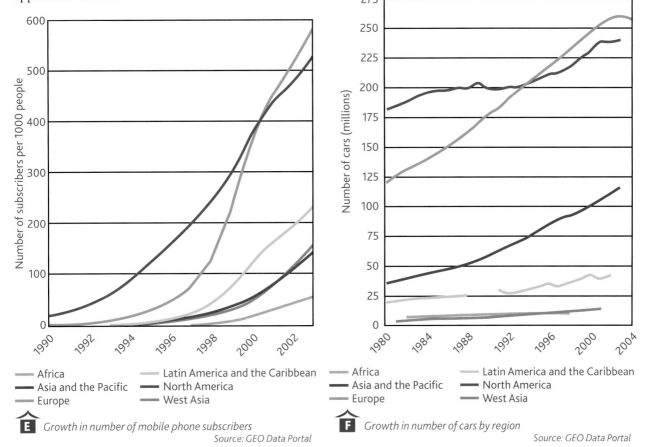

▬ Africa	▬ Latin America and the Caribbean
▬ Asia and the Pacific	▬ North America
▬ Europe	▬ West Asia

E *Growth in number of mobile phone subscribers*

Source: GEO Data Portal

▬ Africa	▬ Latin America and the Caribbean
▬ Asia and the Pacific	▬ North America
▬ Europe	▬ West Asia

F *Growth in number of cars by region*

Source: GEO Data Portal

So far, in every case, as a country has developed economically, that is built more houses, factories, roads, hospitals and so on, it has also:

- needed more land, fertiliser and pesticide to grow food
- needed more water
- burned more fossil fuels like coal
- emitted more carbon dioxide – the main greenhouse gas.

Over the next 20 years, environmental scientists expect populations to grow quickly in most Asian and all African countries. But many scientists are worried that **land degradation**, loss of **biodiversity** and environmental **pollution** will prevent us being able to produce sufficient food. Similarly, many scientists believe that there will not be enough fresh water or non-renewable resources such as fossil fuels to enable LEDCs to develop in the way that countries have in the past.

Key terms

Land degradation: the decrease in the capacity of the land to produce (food) caused by human activity and natural processes, e.g. soil erosion.

Biodiversity: the number and variety of species within a region.

Pollution: undesirable change in the physical, chemical or biological characteristics of land, air and water which can harm the lives of humans and other organisms.

How many people do we need to plan for?

Population scientists have to plan for the expected future population of a country. An increase in a country's human population will mean that more schools and hospitals will be needed and more energy in the form of electricity will be needed, so more power stations or wind farms will be needed. However, it can take 15 years to build a new power station so it is no use waiting until the new individuals have been born.

The first step is to work out the size of the present population. But even counting individuals in a country the size of India is a huge task (see Map **G**).

In India there's 19 times the UK population in an area 12 times bigger. During a census, people are asked to report how many people there are in their family. But some families are missed out, others do not tell the truth or do not return the census form. So even this stage is tricky.

Trying to predict the future size of a country's population is even harder. Even if a country strictly controls immigration, people may simply decide that they want bigger or smaller families than their parents. Medical advances may cut death rates from a particular disease or a war may kill millions in a single year.

The population of a country in 20 years' time is affected by things which are nearly impossible to predict.

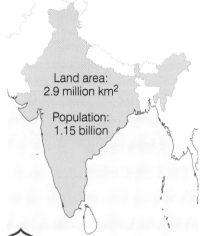

Land area: 2.9 million km^2

Population: 1.15 billion

G   *Can you calculate the population density of India?*

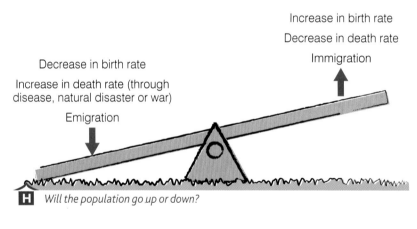

Increase in birth rate
Decrease in death rate
Immigration

Decrease in birth rate
Increase in death rate (through disease, natural disaster or war)
Emigration

H   *Will the population go up or down?*

Table **I** gives figures for the total population of the world between 1950 and 2050.

I   *World population*

Year	1950	1970	1990	2010	2030	2050
Total population in billions	2.5	3.7	5.3	6.8	8.1	8.9

5   **a**   Use figures from Table **I** to copy and complete Graph **J**.

b   Use Graph **J** to estimate the year in which the total population of the world would reach seven billion people.

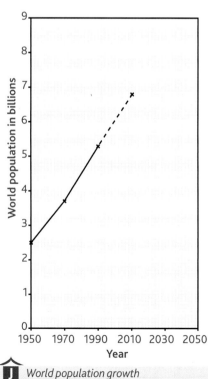

J   *World population growth*

What is an ecological footprint?

The **ecological footprint** is the amount of the Earth's resources in an area that a person or group consumes to support their lifestyle. Diagram **K** shows the components of the ecological footprint of London.

As you can see, to calculate a person's or group's ecological footprint we need to work out how many resources are used up in providing them with food, energy and transport and how many resources it takes to dispose of their wastes.

MEDCs have much bigger ecological footprints than LEDCs.

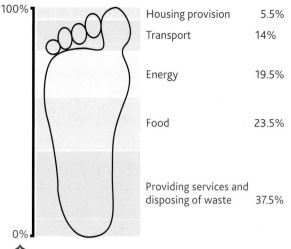

Housing provision	5.5%
Transport	14%
Energy	19.5%
Food	23.5%
Providing services and disposing of waste	37.5%

K   *London's ecological footprint*

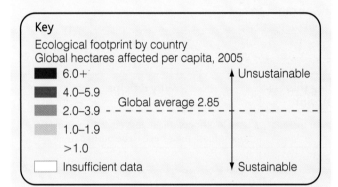

Key

Ecological footprint by country
Global hectares affected per capita, 2005

- 6.0+   ▲ Unsustainable
- 4.0–5.9
- 2.0–3.9   Global average 2.85
- 1.0–1.9
- >1.0
- ☐ Insufficient data   ▼ Sustainable

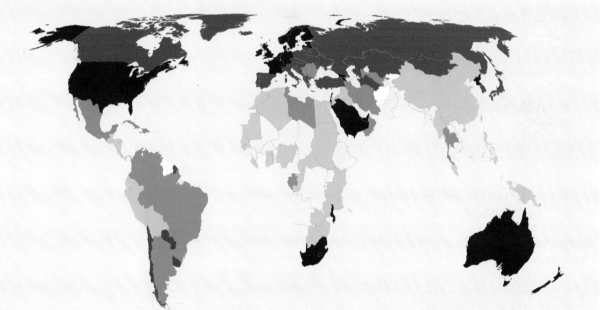

L   *Variations in ecological footprints*
Source: Global Footprint Network

People in LEDCs have few resources – they rarely have modern homes with energy-hungry appliances, they do not have electricity or clean water in their homes and their only form of transport is walking. They have small ecological footprints. As a country develops, it uses more fossil fuels in building, transport and manufacturing goods. Their ecological footprint, or harmful impact on the Earth, increases.

Key terms

Ecological footprint: the amount of the Earth's resources of an area that a person or group consumes to support their lifestyle.

How can environmental scientists reduce our impact?

Many scientists, engineers, economists and politicians are working to try to reduce humans' ecological footprint and plan for a sustainable lifestyle. This involves looking at every aspect of our lives and asking the question: 'How can human activity be changed so that less energy and fewer resources are used?'

Group activity

Working in small groups, copy out the list of everyday activities shown in the table below. For each activity listed in the left-hand column, think of as many ways as you can of changing what we do to reduce the impacts and write them in the second column of your table. In the third column, briefly explain why this change reduces your footprint. Compare your list with other groups to find out who thought of the most ideas or who had original suggestions.

As an example, a few ideas have been written in already.

Activity	Ways of reducing this bit of our footprint	Why it helps
Having a lovely hot, deep bath 3 times a week	Have a quick shower instead of a bath	Uses less hot water so less electricity is used so less fossil fuels need to be burned
Having a bacon sandwich for breakfast	Have cereal instead	
Getting mum to drop you off at the school gate in her 4x4		
Flying to Disneyland for the annual family holiday		
Setting the thermostat to 20 °C and timing it to start at 6.00am so that the house is nice and toasty by the time you get up		
Leaving the bathroom light on all night 'just in case'		
Asking for a new carrier bag every time you buy something at the shop		

Our governments employ environmental scientists to advise them on how the whole country's footprint can be reduced. Each day, households in the UK throw away 3000 tonnes of wasted food. In the past, this was collected by the dustbin men and dumped in a landfill site – literally, a huge hole in the ground. When it rotted, huge amounts of methane, a very powerful greenhouse gas, were released into the atmosphere. This made the greenhouse effect much worse (Section A3.1). Now, many councils are collecting food and green waste separately and composting it. Environmental engineers have developed ways in which the wastes are turned into a useful fertiliser that can be used in parks or sold to make money that the council can use for local services.

We know for certain that fossil fuels will run out so it makes sense to develop renewable energy sources such as wind farms now. As with recycling, consumers need to be encouraged by government financial incentives such as grants and subsidies. All of these changes are necessary in order for us to reduce our harmful impact on the planet.

Activity

Annually in the UK, private companies extract 2.5 Mm³ of peat yet local authorities landfill 4 million tonnes of compostable garden waste. Diagram **M** shows the flow of energy along a food chain.

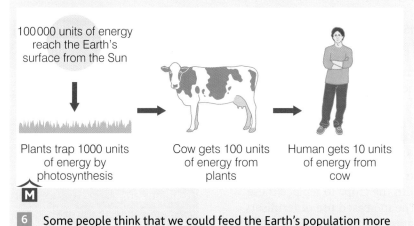

100 000 units of energy reach the Earth's surface from the Sun

Plants trap 1000 units of energy by photosynthesis

Cow gets 100 units of energy from plants

Human gets 10 units of energy from cow

M

6 Some people think that we could feed the Earth's population more efficiently. They think that people should eat less meat and more food from plants. Explain how the food chain diagram could be used to argue in favour of this idea.

Activity

7 Environmental scientists are developing new technologies to help reduce the impact of our waste. Use the internet or textbooks to explain how the following help to reduce the amount of waste we landfill, conserve resources and reduce pollution:

- incineration
- bottle/can/paper recycling.

Summary

Sustainable development is development which meets present needs without compromisng the ability of future generations to achieve their needs and aspirations.

Current population growth appears unsustainable because of pollution, loss of biodiversity, loss of fertile land and the exhaustion of non-renewable resources such as fossil fuels.

Predicting future population sizes is difficult but is essential if we are to build sufficient power stations, hospitals and other services and grow adequate quantities of food.

The ecological footprint is the amount of the Earth's resources in an area that a person or group consumes to support their lifestyle. People in MEDCs have huge footprints compared to people in LEDCs.

We need to reduce our footprint to ensure sustainability. This will include switching to alternative energy sources from fossil fuels and reducing the amount of waste we generate.

How may food supplies be increased to provide for the growing population?

What is agricultural intensification of farming practices?

Agricultural **intensification** involves increasing inputs (e.g. fertilisers, **pesticides**, mechanical energy) into agriculture to increase the amount of food produced, that is higher livestock or crop yields. More and larger machines are used, to prepare the soil, plant and harvest the crop and milk the cows, for example. Field sizes are increased for these big machines and hedges and banks are removed. Fossil fuels power the machines.

When a crop is harvested, the nutrients that it contains, which it absorbed from the soil, are removed with the crop. To replace these nutrients, farmers use soil fertilisers. The increased use of fertilisers containing nitrates, phosphates and potassium dramatically increases food production, see the table below.

A *Fertilisers*

Nutrient	What the farmer applies	Why is the nutrient needed?
Nitrogen (N)	Nitrates	Good leaf growth
Phosphorus (P)	Phosphates	Good root growth
Potassium (K)	Potash	Hardiness and fruit production

Of course, chemical fertilisers like these are not free. The farmer has to work out the best amount to add to his crops. If he tries to save money and uses too little fertiliser, his crops will not grow as well as they could and he will have less product to sell. On the other hand, if he uses more than the crop needs, he will be wasting money – and may harm the crop or cause water pollution.

To increase food production, scientists have also developed ways of reducing the amount of crops that get eaten or damaged by pests and diseases. Pesticides are chemicals designed to kill organisms that harm our crops. By doing this, they help to increase yields even further.

In this section you will learn:

- what is meant by intensification of farming practices
- how agricultural scientists and farmers use controlled environments to increase food production
- about the benefits of selective breeding and genetic manipulation
- about the benefits of improved storage, refrigeration and transport of food
- that the increasing global population means that more food must be grown.

Key terms

Intensification: the use of many inputs (fertiliser, pesticide, mechanisation) in order to increase outputs (food).

Pesticides: chemicals designed to kill organisms that feed on or cause disease in crops, in order to reduce yield losses.

Environmental scientists@work

Golden rice

Professors Ingo Potrykus and Peter Beyer have invented a way of helping to prevent blindness in children. They have been studying the genetics of rice, which is the world's most important staple crop, providing the main source of food for 1.6 billion people. Rice is a good source of energy and fibre but, unfortunately it does not contain any vitamin A. This vitamin is needed to prevent 'night blindness', a condition in which people's eyes do not adjust properly to dim light. The scientists extracted the gene that makes beta-carotene from carrots. They have then inserted the gene into rice. People eating this rice obtain beta-carotene and their bodies can then convert this into vitamin A. This rice is therefore an example of a transgenic organism (see page 36).

B *Ordinary and golden rice*

Agricultural scientists investigated the effect of nitrate fertilisers on the yield of a new variety of wheat. Graph **C** shows their results.

1 A farmer tells the scientists that she has been adding 200 kg of the nitrate fertiliser. What advice should the scientists give her?

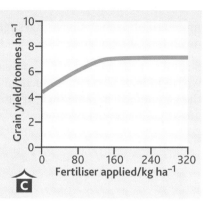

C

Malachy planted 6 seedlings in each of 4 identical plant trays filled with soil. Once a week, for 4 weeks, he added different concentrations of liquid nitrogen fertiliser to each tray. He measured the height of every seedling and worked out the average height for each tray.

1 What variable was Malachy testing?

2 What was the dependent variable?

3 Suggest three precautions Malachy needed to take to ensure it was a fair test.

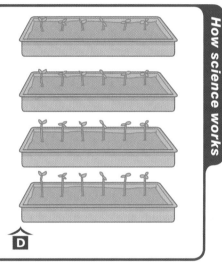

D

How science works

Sitting higher tier

The use of monocultures

One impact of mechanisation is an increase in the use of monoculture – where just one crop is planted over a large area. Having spent a lot of money on a new combine harvester, it makes sense for a farmer to plant as much wheat, for example, as possible. As a result, many farms have become specialised at growing just one or two types of crop.

∞links

Section B2.2 explores how agriculture can cause water pollution.

---

2 Look at this field of wheat (Photo **E**). Make a list of the factors that may have affected how well the wheat has grown.

E

Your list will probably have included factors such as:

- how warm it has been
- whether or not there has been a frost
- whether there has been enough or too much rainfall for a wheat crop
- how the crop has been affected by pests and diseases
- the fertility of the soil
- how much carbon dioxide was available for photosynthesis.

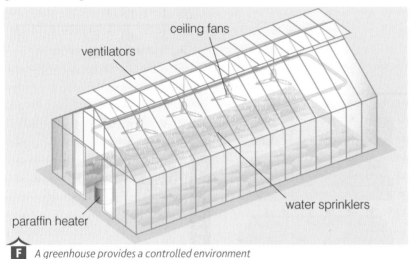

What are controlled environments?

Agricultural scientists have investigated the factors that affect how much food we can grow.

Scientists realised centuries ago that if we could control these factors, we could increase food production. **Controlled environments**, like the greenhouse in Diagram **F**, try to provide the best conditions for the growth of crops and livestock.

ceiling fans

ventilators

water sprinklers

paraffin heater

F *A greenhouse provides a controlled environment*

Activity

3   Copy and complete the table using the words or phrases from the list to explain how a greenhouse provides a controlled environment.

Feature of greenhouse	How it helps to increase plant growth
Glass	
	Prevents greenhouse getting too hot
	Allows precise amount of water or nutrients to be added
Heater	
Lights	

Sprinklers

Allows plants to carry out photosynthesis 24 hours a day if required

Allows temperature to be increased and releases carbon dioxide

Vents and fans

Lets solar radiation in but traps longwave radiation, heating up the air

In battery farms hens are kept in giant sheds in small cages to stop them moving (see Photo **G**). This means they use less energy in respiration and put more of their energy into producing more eggs or meat. The hens are fed precise quantities of high-quality food to optimise their growth. The thousands of hens packed into a confined space generate so much heat through respiration that the owner does not need to spend money artificially heating the shed.

Activity

4   Use the internet or textbooks to make a table listing arguments for and against battery farming of chickens. Consider: animal welfare, wastes, disease, cheap food, protection from predators, taste and any other factors you think are important.

G *Battery farmed hens*

■ What is selective breeding?

Selective breeding occurs when humans intervene in reproduction to decide which individual plants or animals are allowed to breed together. Imagine a farmer wants to produce a lot of attractive, black and white patterned wool (Photo **H**).

H   *A lamb with black and white wool*

She selects two types of sheep to breed from (see Diagram **I**). Breed A produces lots of thick wool, but most of it is black. Breed B produces wool with the desired black and white colouring, but unfortunately does not produce much of it. She allows carefully selected individuals of breed A to mate with selected individuals of breed B. From the offspring she then chooses males and females that have the best combination of thick, black and white-coloured wool and allows them to breed together. After doing this over many generations she ends up with a big flock of sheep that are producing lots of the desired wool.

By carefully choosing which individuals have been allowed to mate humans have, over thousands of years, managed to combine many useful characteristics together in livestock such as cows and sheep and in all of our major food crops to produce more and better food.

I   *Selective breeding*

J   *Aims of selective breeding in different species*

Crop/animal		Desired characteristic
Cow		High milk yield to maximise economic efficiency
Bull		High meat : fat ratio so our meat is healthier to eat
Tomato		Improved taste, uniformity of size and appearance and resistance to disease
Rice		Drought resistance so that we can grow rice in more areas of the wrold

Key terms

Selective breeding: the selection by humans of individuals to breed together, based upon their useful characteristics.

Genetically modified organism: an organism that has had its genetic material altered in a way that does not occur naturally by mating.

What are genetically modified organisms?

A **genetically modified organism** is one that has had its DNA altered in a way that does not occur naturally by mating. It may involve creating a transgenic organism – one that has had a gene from another organism inserted into it (see the example of golden rice on page 32).

Aims of genetic engineering:

- increase growth and yield
- reduce the need for chemical pesticides and herbicides
- reduce water use
- develop plants that are productive in marginal farmland
- increase nutritional quality
- improve flavour and appearance
- improve plant qualities for harvesting, shipping and storage.

How has technology improved storage, refrigeration and transport of food?

Once we have successfully produced food, we need to ensure that it remains edible and does not begin to rot or decay. Decaying food contains microorganisms such as bacteria and fungi. These organisms produce toxins which cause food poisoning if we eat the decaying food.

We have developed many ways of preserving food, some of these are shown in Figure **K**.

 a *Drying*

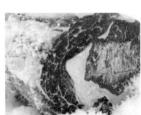

b *Freezing*

c *Canning*

 **d** *Adding salt or sugar*

e *Pickling*

K *Some methods of preserving food, can you think of any more?*

Using these techniques we can transport food all over the world and store grain, for example, for many months before consuming it. Vast refrigeration ships can freeze hundreds of thousands of fish within an hour of them being hauled in. Some of these technologies, irradiation for example, are modern. Others, such as smoking fish, are ancient. And, as we shall see in the next chapter, some are more sustainable and transferable from MEDCs to LEDCs, than others.

Activity

5 Copy and complete the table to show how each food preservation technique works. One has been done for you!

Preservation technique	How it works
	Food is heated to kill microorganisms and sealed in a vacuum
Freezing	Kills most microorganisms and slows down the growth of others by stopping enzymes working
Pickling	
Drying	
	Osmotically pulls out water from the microorganisms, killing them
	The use of electron beams, X-rays or gamma rays to kill bacteria in food

Summary

The intensification of agriculture has involved using more and more fertilisers, pesticides and mechanical inputs and has dramatically increased food production.

Selective breeding, where humans decide which individuals are allowed to mate, is an ancient practice and has been used to combine useful characteristics.

Genetically modified organisms may contain DNA from completely different species. They cannot occur naturally but may be of great use in agriculture.

Technologies such as refrigeration, salting and drying help slow down food decay, increasing the shelf-life of food and enabling us to transport and store food more efficiently.

A1.4 Are the developments in world food production sustainable?

Why are 850 million people hungry?

In 2008, food scientists working for the United Nations World Food Programme estimated that 850 million people were suffering from hunger – that's 14 hungry people for every satisfied person in the UK. In large parts of the world, people do not have enough to eat.

In this section you will learn:

the causes of hunger

how Europe increased food production after World War II

about the "Green Revolution"

about the consequences of the globalisation of food production

about the arguments for and against GM food

about the environmental impacts of food production.

widespread lack of access
shortfall in food production/supplies
severe localised food insecurity

A *Countries requiring food aid*

Source: UNECA 2004

Poverty is the major reason why so many people remain in perpetual hunger. In Africa, the proportion of people living below the poverty line is actually increasing. In 2005, 313 million Africans lived on less than US$1 per day. As a result of inadequate food production, Africa spends US$15–20 billion on food imports annually, in addition to receiving US$2 billion every year in food aid.

Over huge areas of some African countries, **soil degradation** has been caused by the build up of salts, a process known as **salinisation**, and by **erosion**. The amount of fertile arable land available per person is decreasing (see Bar chart **B**). Unable to grow and sell their crops, people who have lost their land descend into poverty. Others simply use the same piece of land over and over again, reducing its fertility until it too is degraded. If Africa is ever to feed itself, millions of hectares of degraded land will need to be made fertile again.

Key terms

Soil degradation: the breakdown and loss of fertility of soil.

Salinisation: the build-up of salts in soil that is toxic to plant roots.

Erosion: the loss of soil as it is washed and blown away.

Pesticides: chemicals designed to kill organisms that feed on or cause disease in crops, in order to reduce yield losses.

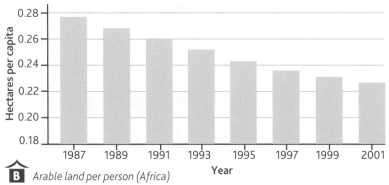

B *Arable land per person (Africa)*

Source: Geo Data Portal

Trees to improve soil quality

Soil scientists in Thailand are investigating whether the fertility of dry, saline soils can be improved by planting salt- and drought-tolerant species of Acacia trees. They have planted 12 plots of three different varieties of Acacia and are monitoring the levels of nitrogen, organic matter and salts in the soil in these areas. It is hoped that the trees will increase the amount of nitrogen and organic matter and reduce the level of salts in the soil. If successful, similar trials are planned for parts of Africa where the soils have been degraded in the same way.

C *Acacia trees in Africa*

Besides poverty, the main causes of hunger include natural disasters such as drought (e.g. in Australia, the Ukraine and Russia), flooding (e.g. in Bangladesh), political instability (e.g. in Zimbabwe) and wars (e.g. in Sudan). Climate change is likely to mean that some regions become much drier or flood more often. The crops grown in these vulnerable areas now will be unable to be grown in much drier or flooded conditions.

Plant scientists are using breeding techniques and genetic manipulation to try to produce varieties of all the major crops (rice, wheat, barley, maize) that will grow in dry or polluted soils.

How did Europe increase food production after World War II?

During World War II (1939–1945), there were widespread food shortages across Europe. After the war, governments demanded that food production should be increased. This was achieved by intensification – the increased use of inputs like machinery, fertilisers and **pesticides** – to get greater outputs, in other words, more food!

Tractors replaced horse-drawn ploughs. Gradually, machines were used to do almost all the tasks that had always previously been done by hand.

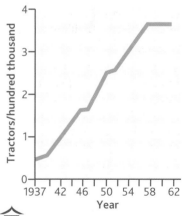

D *Increase in the number of tractors used in agriculture since 1937*

Activity

1   Use the list below to complete the table of inputs and outputs for a dairy farm.

milk   fuel   light   labour   calves   pesticide   water

Inputs	Outputs

AQA *Examiner's tip*

Candidates are often confused about the term 'inputs'. Inputs are just any form of energy that the farmer supplies to the animals or crops.

The mechanisation of agriculture meant that ploughing, seeding, spreading fertilser and pesticide and harvesting could all be done faster and more efficiently. The manufacture of machines, fertiliser and pesticides involves burning fossil fuels but larger areas of land could be cultivated and food production increased rapidly.

Governments encouraged farmers to intensify by offering them subsidies or guaranteed minimum prices for their products. No matter how much milk and grain the farmers produced, the government would guarantee to pay them a fixed, high price for it all. Along with generous loans to buy new machinery, this encouraged farmers to produce more and more food.

What was the 'Green Revolution'?

In the 1950s, scientists turned their attention to the problem of how to feed the rapidly growing populations of some countries in Asia. The 'Green Revolution' that resulted involved the breeding of high-yielding varieties of seed for crops such as wheat, sorghum and rice, and a huge increase in the use of fertilisers, pesticides and irrigation. The 'Green Revolution' also involved education programmes aimed at teaching farmers how to improve crop growth and it certainly increased food production in Asia dramatically. However, as you can see in Graph **E**, there has been no 'Green Revolution' in Africa.

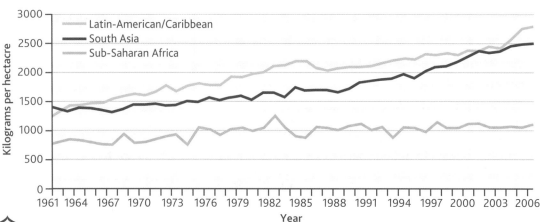

E Changes in grain yield per hectare in sub-Saharan Africa, South Asia and Latin America/Caribbean

Source: Food and Agriculture Organization of the UN, www.fao.org

The International Rice Research Institute (IRRI) in the Philippines employs hundreds of scientists, all working to improve the quantity and quality of rice. Rice is grown in 114 countries and is the main source of food for millions of people. In 2007, 645 million tonnes of rice were grown!

In 1962 the IRRI launched a rice breeding programme. At that time, the average rice yield in South East Asia was 1500 kg per hectare. By 1965, the IRRI scientists had developed semi-dwarf, stiff-strawed, disease-resistant varieties that grew extremely well when given plenty of fertiliser. One variety yielded 9000 kg per hectare. Asian farmers called them miracle plants, but they were actually the result of plant scientists working together intensively.

Environmental scientists@work

Activity

The 'Green Revolution' involved developing crop varieties that grew extremely quickly as long as they were given large amounts of fertilisers. These fertilisers are expensive and can only be manufactured using large amounts of fossil fuels.

2 Suggest why some scientists believed that the 'Green Revolution' was an unsustainable approach to the need for increased food production.

What are the consequences of the globalisation of food production?

Every day, millions of tonnes of food are shipped and flown around the world. Your local supermarket will have green beans flown in from Kenya, bacon from Holland, lamb chops from New Zealand and bananas from the Cayman Islands. There are benefits and problems associated with this globalisation.

On the positive side, we are able to choose from a huge range of foodstuffs, including many healthy types of vegetables and fruit when our own varieties are out of season. By purchasing green beans grown in Kenya, we also provide farmers, their families and local villages with much-needed income.

However, it may also mean that poor farmers in LEDCs choose or are forced to grow crops for export to MEDCs rather than grow their own food. This means that they must buy more of their everyday foods and this demand may lead to the prices of these staples increasing.

Flying green beans in from Kenya emits a lot of harmful carbon dioxide into the atmosphere. It adds a lot to our ecological footprint. Some scientists believe that we should try just to eat locally grown food. However, other scientists disagree. They point out that Kenyan farmers use only manual labour – they do not have tractors – and the only fertiliser they use is manure from cattle. Your local farmer will almost certainly use machinery that burns fossil fuels, emitting carbon dioxide. The **artificial fertilisers** and pesticides they use are made using enormous amounts of fossil fuels. So the carbon emissions calculation is not as straightforward as it first appears.

F *Supermarket food comes from all over the world*

Key terms

Artificial fertilisers: nitrates, phosphates and potassium that are added to the soil to increase crop growth.

Food miles: the distance food travels through the complete production process until it reaches the consumer.

Activity

3 Work out how many **food miles** were involved in a typical dinner at your house. You'll need to identify where the food came from by looking on the wrapper or the sign in the supermarket (see Photo **F** for an example). Then, use an atlas or the internet to calculate how many miles each part of the meal has travelled to get to your plate.

⬭links

Go online and read the article by Robin McKie 'How the myth of food miles hurts the planet.' *Observer*, Sunday 23 March, 2008

www.guardian.co.uk/ environment/2008/mar/23/food. ethicalliving

Sitting higher tier

What are the arguments for and against GM food?

GM food is a highly controversial topic! Some scientists believe that growing GM crops is the only way that we are going to feed the growing human population. They argue that it would be unethical not to grow them. Other scientists argue just the opposite. They believe that GM crops could damage the environment and human health. Some countries have planted millions of hectares of land with GM crops, but most have been extremely cautious.

G   *Arguments for and against GM food*

Arguments for GM food	Arguments against GM food
Increases food production when millions are starving	Little evidence that GM crops do increase food production
Reduces the amount of land used for food production, leaving more for other uses	If GM crops are not more productive, then this argument is false
Transgenic plants (those that contain genes from other organisms) do not survive long in the wild so there is little chance that they will pollinate weeds to create super-weeds	Scientists have shown that GM genes have transferred to weeds growing near to the GM crops. This could lead to super-weeds. If altered genes spread, it could make organic farming impossible.
GM food contains just the same type of nutrients as non-GM food so it should be safe to eat	There have been almost no scientific investigations on the effects of eating GM food so we can not be sure that there won't be long-term harmful effects on health, e.g. allergies
Can mean longer shelf-life for certain products so reducing need for refrigeration which generates carbon dioxide	Reducing food miles is a better way of reducing the ecological footprint of food storage and distribution
GM crops can be made to be salt and drought-tolerant	It would be better to clean up saline soils and use irrigation to provide water
Plants can be adapted to absorb fertiliser more efficiently	Fertilisers are made using fossil fuels that will run out. It would be better to use organic techniques
Farmers growing crops genetically modified to produce toxins to pests use less insecticide and suffer fewer cases of insecticide poisoning	It is just a matter of time before the insects develop resistance to the toxin
The technology is relatively simple and easy to use in LEDCs	GM technology is owned by a few giant companies in MEDCs – small farmers in India should not have to depend on them and shouldn't have to buy new seed each year

H   *GM crop growth by country*

Country	Area of GM crops/ millions of hectares
USA	47.6
Argentina	16.2
Canada	5.4
Brazil	5.0
China	3.7
Paraguay	1.2
India	0.5
South Africa	0.5
Uruguay	0.3
Australia	0.2
All other countries	0.4

Activity

4   Can you suggest why there have been almost no studies into the health effects of eating GM food?

What are the environmental impacts of food production?

Imagine that you are standing, 300 years, ago, where Photo I was taken. What would be different? The answer is just about everything. You would probably be surrounded by trees since, over most of England, deciduous woodland is the natural ecosystem. The English countryside that we love – green fields with dry stone walls, heather moorlands, downlands, hay meadows and ponds – are all artificial.

Most of the woodland was chopped down and burned and most naturally wet areas were drained to make way for crops and pasture. This destroyed the habitats of many organisms leading to a loss of biodiversity.

I *Wheat monoculture in Warwickshire*

The increasing use of fertilisers and pesticides after World War II also caused serious problems. Nitrates and phosphates found their way into streams, ponds and lakes. The addition of excess nutrients into water is called **eutrophication**. The nutrients stimulated the growth of microscopic plants called algae, which spread like a green blanket across the surface of the water. When these plants died, they were broken down by bacteria. These bacteria used up all of the oxygen in the water, killing just about everything else that lived in the water.

Pesticides intended to kill crop pests ended up killing birds of prey instead. Sometimes, useful insects such as ladybirds or pollinating wasps were also accidentally killed by these chemicals. The organisms that normally fed on these insects suddenly lost their food source and food chains were disrupted.

Soil that had formed over hundreds of thousands of years was quickly washed away by rainfall if farmers cleared vegetation from steep slopes or left the ground bare after harvest. Even GM crops need soil! These impacts are discussed further in Chapters B1 and B2.

Summary

The main causes of hunger are poverty, drought, flooding, war and political unrest.

MEDCs have increased food production by mechanising their agriculture and by using huge amounts of fertilisers and pesticides.

The Green Revolution refers to the huge increases in crop production in Asia made possible by agricultural education and the use of high-yielding varieties, fertilisers, pesticides and irrigation.

Globalisation means that consumers in MEDCs have a huge range of foods from all over the world to choose from. Farmers in LEDCs get valuable income.

GM food remains highly controversial.

Agriculture has been responsible for serious environmental damage including habitat destruction, water pollution and soil erosion.

Activity

5 The table shows the total energy input (in the form of fuel for machinery, seeds, fertilisers and pesticides) and yield per hectare for commercial rice cultivation in the USA and traditional rice cultivation in Vietnam.

	Commercial rice production in the US	Traditional rice cultivation in Vietnam
Energy input/10^6 J per hectare	65 000	175
Yield/kg per hectare	5 800	1280

a For each country, calculate the yield of rice obtained per joule of energy supplied.

b State which country's rice production is more efficient.

c Which system is more sustainable? Explain your answer.

A2.1 How are energy resources used?

How do we use energy resources?

Energy is one of our most precious and vital resources. We rely on energy to support our lifestyles and our economic prosperity. Most of the time we take it for granted that energy will be available for whatever we want, whenever we want it.

We use energy in lots of different ways (see Photos **A**).

In this section you will learn:

how energy is used in the modern world

how energy consultants and individuals can monitor energy consumption

how energy consumption has changed with our changing lifestyles.

A Energy at home, on the move, at work and for leisure

Environmental scientists@work

How much does your radio cost to run?

Electronics experts working for Efergy have invented a simple device that they claim will help every household save electricity – and money.

Their wireless electricity meter tells you exactly how much electricity any appliance is using, how much it is costing per minute and even how much CO_2 is being generated when its on.

It will probably encourage you to turn things off at the wall!

⬭links

Visit **www.efergy.com** to find out more.

Activity

1. Draw a spider diagram or mind map to show how you and your family use energy at home, in transport, at work and school and for any other activities including leisure and recreation.

B A gas meter and an electricity meter

How can we monitor energy consumption?

Most homes, businesses and public buildings (including schools) are supplied with gas and electricity to provide energy. A gas **meter** measures the amount of gas that is used and there is another meter for electricity. These meters give individuals and **energy consultants** the information they need to monitor the amount of energy being used.

The gas and electricity meters in houses are usually hidden away in a cupboard but the supply companies regularly send people to read the meters and you should be able to find out where yours are. In school, the caretakers or the premises manager will know where the meters are.

To make it easier for people to monitor their electricity consumption at home some people now use a wireless energy monitor. A sensor is clipped onto the supply cable which brings electricity into the house. This detects how much electricity is being used and transmits this information to a hand-held display. With one of these monitors you can see instantly how much electricity is used when particular appliances are switched on (and how much is saved when they are turned off). The display also shows the cost of the electricity being used.

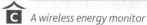

C A wireless energy monitor

links

There is more information about how individuals and **energy consultants** can use information about energy use in the next section, A2.2.

Activities

2 Use meter readings from your own home to monitor the amount of gas and electricity your family uses on a daily basis. Record your readings. What causes the consumption to go up or down? Is your consumption similar on weekdays and at weekends? Does the temperature outside have an effect?

3 Find out whether your school or college keeps records of the amount of gas and electricity used every day; if not then see if you can arrange for daily readings to be taken and recorded for you to use. (Some schools use oil rather than gas for heating.)

4 Investigate how the amount of energy used at home or school changes with the temperature. Plot results for temperature and energy use on a graph. Which variable will you plot on the vertical (*y*) axis? Why?

links

Check out the guidance on dependent and independent variables in the How Science Works section on pages 8–9 if you aren't sure about this.

How has energy use changed?

We use far more energy in our day-to-day lives than people did in the past. Illustration **D** shows an Iron Age village around 2000 years ago. Think about the lives of the people who lived in the village. What energy resources would they have used? How would they have heated their homes? How would they have cooked their food? How would they have got around? What would they have done for entertainment? We do not have to go back 2000 years to find a time when people used far less energy than they do now. Just 50 years ago people's lifestyles used far less energy than today.

D *An Iron Age village*

Activity

5   Interview someone you know who is over 60 years old (grandparents or great-grandparents would be ideal). Find out how your interviewee's home was heated when they were your age – did they have central heating and, if not, how many rooms were heated in winter? Did their family have a car, and if not how did they get around? Did they take plane flights for holidays or work? What electrical appliances did they have?

Group activity

As a class, you could build up a more reliable picture of energy use in the past by designing a questionnaire with standard questions, getting every member of the class to find someone to complete it. Then write a report including an analysis of the results, with calculations of totals, means and percentages.

Why have we used more and more energy? The major reason is that the world population has increased rapidly. More people means more energy-consuming cars, houses, factories and appliances. Energy analysts expect energy consumption to continue to grow, at least for the next 20 years see Graph **E**. However, many scientists are worried that at some point this trend will have to change – this will be discussed in more detail in Section A2.3.

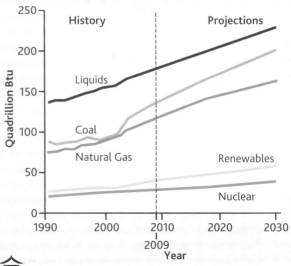

E *The increasing amount of energy used by humans*
Source: Energy Information Administration (EIA), www.eia.doe.gov/iea

Energy use in different countries

As well as differences in energy use between the past and the present, there are also big differences between the lifestyles and the energy consumption of people living in different countries today (see Map **F**).

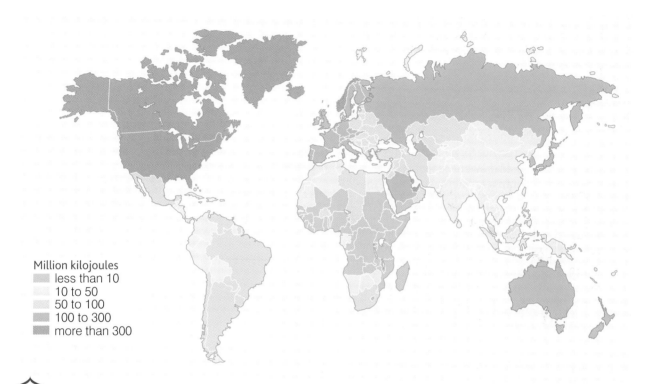

Million kilojoules
- less than 10
- 10 to 50
- 50 to 100
- 100 to 300
- more than 300

F Energy consumption per head of population in different countries

Activities

6   Look at Map **F**. Why has energy use per head been mapped rather than the total amount of energy used in each country?

7   Copy out the following sentences, and complete them by choosing the correct words and phrases when you are given a choice.

The countries where people use the most energy are mainly in the <u>northern/southern</u> parts of the world.

<u>Africa/Asia</u> is the continent where people generally use the smallest amounts of energy.

The continent where people use the largest amounts of energy is <u>Europe/North America</u>.

8   Use an atlas to help you identify the following:

a   a country in North America where people used an average of 10–50 million kilojoules per person in 2004

b   countries in the southern hemisphere where people used an average of over 150 million kilojoules per person

c   the country in southern Africa with the highest level of energy consumption.

Testing the hypothesis that energy consumption is higher in richer countries

Tom and Sara set out to test the hypothesis that energy consumption is higher in richer countries (More Economically Developed Countries – MEDCs) and lower in poorer countries (Less Economically Developed Countries – LEDCs). They chose 12 countries and found the figures in Table **G** from the internet.

Activities

9 Plot the figures from Table **G** on a scatter graph. Plot GDP on the horizontal axis. Give your graph a title and do not forget to label the axes properly. You could draw the graph by hand or put the data into a spreadsheet and use the graph function to produce the graph. If you use a computer you will still need to think about a title and the labels for the axes: you can not just rely on the software to do the whole job for you.

10 Look at your completed graph and then write a conclusion to this investigation. Do the results give strong support to Tom and Sara's hypothesis, do they only give partial support or do they suggest that the hypothesis is false?

11 Can you suggest any possible limitations of this investigation which may affect how reliable it is as a test of Tom and Sara's hypothesis? (Think about what you know, or do not know, about how Tom and Sara chose the countries in the table. How many countries did they investigate? How many are there in the whole world? What do you know about where the data came from?) Sampling methods, sample size and reliability of secondary data are all important factors to think about when you are planning an investigation.

G

Country	Energy used in toe* per person per year	GDP** in $US per person per year
Bangladesh	0.2	400
Brazil	1.1	5000
China	1.2	2000
France	4.5	35000
India	0.5	700
Ivory Coast	0.4	900
Japan	4.2	35000
Mexico	1.6	7000
Nepal	0.3	300
South Africa	2.8	5000
United Kingdom	3.9	37000
United States	7.9	42000

* toe stands for tonnes of oil equivalent – the amount of energy used is calculated as if it were all obtained from oil.
** GDP stands for Gross Domestic Product – the total value of goods and services produced within a country.

Activities

12 List four different ways in which you use energy resources at home.

13 What is an electricity meter?

14 Explain why people in MEDCs use more energy than people in LEDCs.

15 Briefly describe the work of an energy consultant.

Summary

In the modern world, we use energy resources in almost every aspect of our lives.

The amount of energy used at home, school or work can be monitored by taking regular readings from gas and electricity meters.

The amount of energy used has increased over the years, but there are still big differences in energy use between the richest countries and the poorest ones.

A2.2 | How can energy consumption be reduced?

■ How can the energy efficiency of our homes be improved?

Many of us want to reduce the amount of energy we use. This may be because we want to cut our bills or because we want to help the environment.

One way to reduce energy consumption is to buy appliances which are more efficient. Most new electrical items, including fridges and fridge-freezers, washing machines, electric tumble dryers, dishwashers, lamps, electric ovens and air conditioners, must have a **European Community energy label** which gives information about energy efficiency.

Changing from old-fashioned incandescent light bulbs to modern energy-saving ones is another simple way of saving energy. The UK government aims to phase out most old-fashioned light bulbs by 2011, although many people will still have them in their homes. The new bulbs cost more, but they only use about 25 per cent of the electricity and they can last up to twelve times as long as old-fashioned ones. An energy-saving bulb can save up to £60 worth of electricity over its lifetime, as well as reducing the emissions of carbon dioxide from burning less fossil fuels.

Environmental scientists@work

Some of the most energy-efficient products have been identified by the Energy Saving Trust and are marked with the Energy Saving Recommended logo, see illustration **C**. If you're shopping for a new dishwasher, boiler or even just light bulbs, always look for the Energy Saving Recommended logo. It's your guarantee that these products have met the strict criteria on energy efficiency, will cost less to run and help reduce carbon emissions. For more information, visit **www.energysavingtrust.org.uk**.

In this section you will learn:

how energy consumption can be reduced by:

* using the most energy-efficient devices
* making sure that homes are insulated and draught-proofed
* making changes to lifestyles.

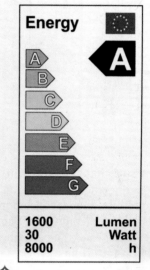

A *A European Community energy label*

B *A conventional and an energy-saving light bulb*

C *Energy Saving Recommended logo*

Key terms

European Community energy label: a label showing how energy-efficient an electrical device is. These labels must appear on most household electrical items sold in the EU. They are intended to help buyers choose the most efficient devices.

Activity

Sophie's parents want to buy a new fridge. Sophie tells them that there's no need, as the old one works fine. They insist, so she tries to persuade them to get the most efficient one possible. They finally have to choose between two models that are the same size and capacity. Diagram **D** shows the labels from the two fridges.

Sophie's dad wants to buy fridge B because it's cheaper. Sophie shows her mum a leaflet from the Energy Saving Trust that tells them that 1 unit of electricity costs 18p. Sophie starts to do a quick calculation:

Fridge	Amount of energy it uses in one year/ units of electricity	Cost of each unit of electricity/ pence	Cost of using the fridge for one year/£
A	275	0.18	49.50
B			

1 Complete Sophie's calculation to show how much they would save on electricity bills in a year if they bought fridge A.

Fridge A

Energy Model A	Fridge £190
More efficient	
A	**A**
B	
C	
D	
E	
Less efficient	
Energy consumption per year	275 kWh

Fridge B

Energy Model B	Fridge £165
More efficient	
A	
B	**B**
C	
D	
E	
Less efficient	
Energy consumption per year	325 kWh

D

Making sure that appliances are replaced with the most energy efficient models on the market can help to reduce energy consumption and buildings can also be made more energy efficient. Diagram **E** shows estimates of the percentage heat loss by different routes from a typical house. It also shows some of the methods which can be used to reduce these losses.

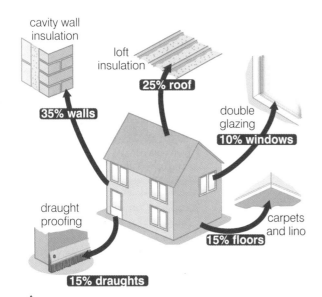

E *Heat is lost from our homes in a number of ways*

cavity wall insulation

loft insulation

25% roof

35% walls

double glazing

10% windows

draught proofing

carpets and lino

15% floors

15% draughts

Thermal imaging

Energy consultants use **thermal imaging surveys** to show where most heat is being lost from buildings. These cameras detect infrared radiation, rather than visible light. The images they produce usually show cold surfaces in blue and green and warm ones in yellow, orange and red.

F *A thermal image of a house*

G *A thermal imaging camera*

Key terms

Thermal Imaging Survey: a survey using a camera which detects infrared radiation rather than visible light. Energy consultants use these cameras to find out where most heat is being lost from buildings.

Activity

2 Look at the thermal image of a house in Photo **F** and then answer the questions below.

a Do you think that this house needs more insulation for the main part of its roof? Explain your answer.

b In their report to the home owner, the energy consultants said that there were problems with most of the window frames in the house. Do you agree with this statement? Explain your answer.

c The consultants' report also said 'We recommend that you improve the insulation in the walls of all the upstairs rooms in the house. This should be an urgent priority.' Do you agree with this or do you think there may have been a mistake when the report was being prepared? Explain your answer.

What are pay-back times and how are they calculated?

One important thing that people think about when they are deciding whether to carry out energy-saving improvements to their homes is the **pay-back time**. The pay-back time for an energy-saving measure is the amount of time it takes to pay for itself through savings on energy costs.

$$\text{Pay-back time (in years)} = \frac{\text{Cost of installing energy-saving measure}}{\text{Annual saving in energy cost}}$$

Key terms

Pay-back time: the amount of time it takes for an energy-saving measure to pay for itself through savings on energy costs.

Activity

3 Copy and complete the table, which shows estimated costs, fuel-bill savings and pay-back times for some energy-saving home improvements.

	Cavity wall insulation	Loft Insulation		Draught proofing
		Adding 200 mm of insulation to an existing 50 mm	Installing 250 mm of insulation where none is currently fitted	
Cost (professionally installed)	£600	£250	£280	£100
Fuel bill saving per year	£120		£140	
Pay-back time in years	5	6.25		4

How can lifestyle changes help reduce energy consumption?

There are lifestyle changes that can be made to cut down the amount of energy used. There are some suggestions here, but you should be able to think of lots more.

- Turn down the central heating thermostat by a couple of degrees. An extra sweater may be needed but energy and money will be saved.
- Spend less time under the shower.
- Turn off TVs and other gadgets when not in use. (Between 5 and 10 per cent of all electricity used in homes in rich countries is wasted by devices left on standby.)
- Switch lights off when a room is empty.
- Use the car less – walk, cycle or use public transport more.
- Recycle and re-use rather than throwing things into the dustbin.
- Grow food in the garden – cut down on wasteful food miles.

◯◯ links

More information about how to save energy can be found at the Energy Saving Trust **www.est.org.uk**

Activity

4 The drawing shows the parts of a house where it is possible to reduce the amount of energy lost.

Give one way in which the amount of energy lost can be reduced from each of the following parts of the house.

   a 1, 2 and 4   b 5   c 7.

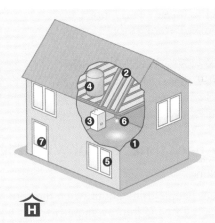

1 walls
2 roof
3 boiler
4 hot water tank
5 window
6 light bulb
7 door

Summary

Many people want to reduce the amount of energy used. This may be to cut bills or to help the environment.

Energy can be saved in a variety of ways, including improvements to the insulation and draught-proofing of homes, buying more energy-efficient appliances and making changes to lifestyles.

When deciding whether to carry out energy-saving improvements people consider the pay-back time. This is the amount of time the improvement takes to pay for itself through savings on energy costs.

Energy consultants carry out surveys and give advice on how to save energy.

A2.3 Why is the continued use of fossil fuels unsustainable?

▇ Are we using fossil fuels too quickly?

Fossil fuels are burnt to produce heat for industry, to heat people's homes, to provide power for transport and to produce electricity. The main fossil fuels are coal, oil (petroleum) and natural gas. They are all formed from organic matter which became buried under layers of sediment and then altered by intense heat and pressure over millions of years.

- **Coal** was formed from the remains of trees and other plants which grew in swamps mainly in the Carboniferous Period, between 280 and 370 million years ago (see Diagram **A**).

- **Oil** (petroleum) was also formed from the remains of living organisms, mainly phytoplankton – tiny single-celled plants – living in the sea. When these organisms died they drifted down and became part of the fine, muddy sediment that built up on the sea bed. As more and more sediment accumulated, it became compressed to form mudstone and shale. The pressure of the rock above and heat from the interior of the Earth gradually 'cooked' the organic matter in these sea-floor deposits and oil was formed.

- **Natural gas** is often found with oil, and also in coal seams. Natural gas is mainly made up of methane, which is given off by anaerobic bacteria (bacteria which are able to live without oxygen) breaking down some of the organic matter which formed oil and coal. Most of the gas that is extracted for use is found close to oilfields. The methane released from coal seams causes dangerous explosions in underground mines and so it was seen as a problem, but energy companies are working on ways to use this coal seam gas.

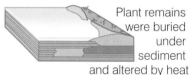

Trees die in swampy forest during the Carboniferous Period.

Plant remains were buried under sediment and altered by heat and pressure...

...forming coal.

A *Coal formation*

Key terms

Fossil fuels: these are fuels formed from the remains of dead plants and animals. The three main fossil fuels are coal, oil and natural gas. They were formed millions of years ago.

Activity

1

a Plot the data from Table **B** on a graph. Plot three line graphs on the same set of axes. Use different colours for each line.

b Describe the trends shown by your completed graph.

c People have been worried that fossil fuels are being used too quickly since at least the early 1970s. Do the data in the table suggest that anything has been done about this? Explain your answer.

B *World consumption of fossil fuels, 1965 to 2007*

	Consumption of fossil fuels		
	Coal/ mtoe*	Oil/ millions of tonnes	Natural gas/mtoe*
1965	1482	1531	598
1970	1534	2254	908
1975	1613	2679	1082
1980	1809	2980	1309
1985	2076	2808	1501
1990	2229	3155	1788
1995	2286	3264	1936
2000	2340	3559	2199
2005	2892	3871	2497
2007	3178	3953	2638

*mtoe = millions of tonnes of oil equivalent – the amount of oil which would have to be burned to provide the same amount of energy as was obtained from the coal or natural gas
Source: BP Statistical Review of World Energy 2008

Fossil fuels took millions of years to form but since the Industrial Revolution they have been used more quickly. This means that sooner or later fossil fuels will run out (or at least become too difficult and expensive to find and extract from the ground). This is why fossil fuels are often called non-renewable resources. No one knows when the fossil fuels will run out, but there is clearly a need to plan for when they do!

■ How does the combustion of fossil fuels cause pollution?

When fossil fuels are burnt (**combustion**), polluting gases are released into the atmosphere. The main pollutants are carbon dioxide, sulfur dioxide and oxides of nitrogen. Products of incomplete combustion such as carbon monoxide and particulates are also produced. Each of these can cause serious environmental problems.

C *Negatve effects of combustion gases*

Gas	Environmental problem
Carbon dioxide	It is a greenhouse gas, trapping heat in the atmosphere. The global climate change that results may cause sea levels to rise, flooding to occur, more catastrophic storms and damage to wildlife habitats
Sulfur dioxide	It dissolves in moisture in the atmosphere to make acid rain. This kills forests and turns lakes and oceans acidic, killing wildlife
Oxides of nitrogen	Along with sulfur dioxide, these also cause acid rain. They also act as greenhouse gases and are associated with photochemical smog

Many scientists believe that global climate change threatens the way in which plant and animal species interact and could lead to the extinction of some species. This could be catastrophic for humans too. If, for example, many insect species were threatened, this might result in much less crop pollination. Without insects such as bees, we would only be able to produce a tiny fraction of the food we produce now. This is another reason why our current use of fossil fuels may be **unsustainable**.

⬭links

Section A3.1 covers greenhouse gases.

Key terms

Combustion: burning.

Unsustainable: a resource is being used unsustainably if it is being used faster than it can be formed again (in other words if it is a non-renewable resource) or if using the resource produces harmful waste or pollution.

Activity

Joe told his dad to turn the television off at the socket rather than leaving it on standby at night to help stop people starving to death in Africa. His dad said he was talking nonsense, because these things weren't connected. Joe drew his dad a flow chart to show he was right.

2 The list below shows Joe's sentences but they have been jumbled up in the wrong order. Copy out the sentences in the right order to explain Joe's argument.

- ▦ less electricity needed
- ▦ less carbon dioxide and oxides of nitrogen released
- ▦ less crop failure
- ▦ turn television off at the socket
- ▦ less drought in parts of Africa
- ▦ less coal burned in the power stations
- ▦ people less likely to starve

Is coal the right option?

In order to help meet growing demand for energy, the government have announced that they intend to build a new coal-fired power station in Kent. Friends of the Earth, an environmental group, are opposed to this plan. They believe that increased use of coal is unsustainable. They have hired a team of chemists to study emissions of sulfur dioxide from a similar coal-burning power station in France. The scientists measured levels of sulfur dioxide at different distances from the power station, including in a city 80 km from the power station (see Diagram D). They also recorded the weather conditions. Complete Activity 3 to discover what they found out.

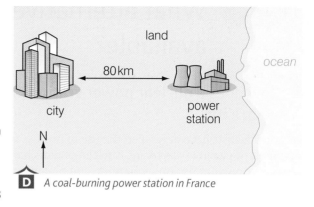

D   *A coal-burning power station in France*

Activities

3   Read the Environmental Scientists@Work box above. Table **E** shows the results Friends of the Earth recorded.

a   Suggest two reasons why Friends of the Earth believe that increased use of coal is unsustainable.

b   Why have the scientists chosen to measure sulfur dioxide?

c   Under what weather conditions might people living in the city be at risk of high sulfur dioxide levels?

d   What do these results tell us about the way sulfur dioxide is transported in the atmosphere?

4

a   Name the three main fossil fuels.

b   Describe how fossil fuels are formed.

c   Explain why fossil fuels are non-renewable resources.

d   List the main pollutants given off when fossil fuels are burned.

E   *Friends of the Earth's study*

Date	Sulfur dioxide concentration in city air/ ppm	Weather conditions
20 September	2.8	Wind: blowing from east to west
		Clear and sunny
22 September	1.7	Wind: blowing from south-east to north-west
		Clear
23 September	0.4	Wind: blowing from west to east
		Heavy rain
24 September	0.2	Wind: blowing from north to south
		Heavy rain
25 September	0.3	Wind: blowing from north to south
		Rain

Summary

The main fossil fuels are coal, oil (petroleum) and natural gas. They are all formed from organic matter which became buried under layers of sediment and then altered by heat and pressure over millions of years.

The continued use of fossil fuels is unsustainable because fuels are being used faster than they can be formed and the combustion of fossil fuels adds to air pollution.

Large amounts of fossil fuels are burnt in power stations to generate electricity. They are also used to produce heat for industry, to heat people's homes and to provide power for transport.

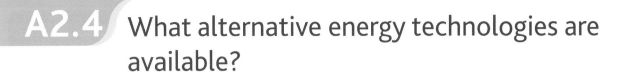

A2.4 What alternative energy technologies are available?

How does a nuclear power station produce electricity?

Nuclear scientists have developed the use of nuclear fuels instead of fossil fuels to generate electricity. Nuclear reactors harness the energy released by **nuclear fission** of uranium and plutonium (see Diagram **A**).

A neutron is fired at a uranium atom...

...which makes the nucleus unstable...

...so that it splits into two smaller nuclei.

The process also releases energy and more neutrons which can carry on the chain reaction.

A *The process of nuclear fission*

The process of nuclear fission releases huge amounts of energy. If this happens very quickly then a nuclear explosion happens, but scientists have been able to develop nuclear reactors (Diagram **B** and Table **C**) which control the rate of the fission reaction so that the energy can be used to generate electricity for peaceful purposes.

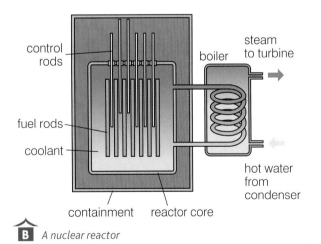

control rods, boiler, steam to turbine, fuel rods, coolant, hot water from condenser, containment, reactor core

B *A nuclear reactor*

In this section you will learn:

how science and technology have been applied to obtain energy from sources other than fossil fuels. This includes:

- how nuclear power stations produce electricity
- how energy can be harnessed from renewable sources
- advantages and disadvantages of the use of fossil fuels, nuclear power, biofuels, tidal power, solar power and wind power.

Key terms

Nuclear fission: the splitting of atoms to release vast amounts of energy.

C *Components of a nuclear reactor*

Component	Description
Control rods	If they are lowered into the reactor they absorb neutrons and slow down the reaction; pull them out and the reaction speeds up.
Containment	Concrete 'shell' designed to prevent radiation leaks.
Reactor core	The 'heart' of the reactor – a sealed container containing the fuel rods, control rods and coolant.
Fuel rods	Metal tubes containing the uranium or plutonium fuel.
Coolant	The coolant circulates through the reactor core and cools it down – the heat is used to boil water in the boiler; the boiling water makes steam which is used to turn a turbine connected to a generator for electricity.

The nuclear reactor in a nuclear power station simply provides the heat to boil water and produce steam. The steam turns turbines which are connected to generators in the same way as in a coal-fired power station. The only thing which is really different about a nuclear power station is the method which is used to boil the water.

What are the advantages and disadvantages of nuclear power?

Some people believe that nuclear power is needed and that it has important advantages, but many others are against further development and use of this technology. Table **D** shows some of the main arguments on both sides. At the time that this textbook is being written it seems likely that the government of the UK will decide that new nuclear power stations should be built in this country, but we can expect to see a major debate about this. Look out for new developments in this area.

D   *Arguments for and against nuclear power*

Advantages	Disadvantages
Nuclear power releases little carbon dioxide, except from fossil fuels used in the manufacture of the station and support of the infrastructure. Therefore it does not add to the greenhouse effect and global climate change.	Nuclear reactors were originally developed to make plutonium for nuclear weapons, therefore some people think it is morally or ethically wrong.
Nuclear power does not give off oxides of sulfur or nitrogen therefore it does not add to acid rain.	The waste produced by nuclear reactors is dangerous because it is radioactive and will continue to be so for thousands of years.
Nuclear reactions release large amounts of energy from small amounts of fuel therefore reducing the impacts of mining and transport of fuel.	There have been accidents at nuclear reactors (e.g. Chernobyl) so many people believe that this makes nuclear power too much of a risk.

E   *The damaged Chernobyl reactor*

Activity

1   Use the internet to research and write a report on nuclear accidents. You should find out about the Windscale fire in 1957, Three Mile Island in 1979 and Chernobyl in 1986 (Photo **E**).

How is energy harnessed from renewable sources?

Scientists have developed sustainable methods of generating electricity from renewable resources which can be used instead of fossil fuels or nuclear power.

Most renewable resources, for example, solar power or wind power are not depleted by their use. The Sun will stop shining sometime in the distant future, but whether the Sun's energy is used on Earth will not affect how long it lasts.

Key terms

Nuclear fusion: the process that occurs in the Sun, when extremely high temperatures cause atoms to join together, releasing vast amounts of energy.

Renewable technology		Description
Solar	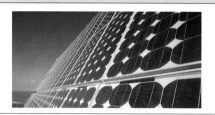	The Sun generates energy via **nuclear fusion**. Solar energy can be: • used to heat water or air which can then be pumped around buildings • converted directly into electricity by photovoltaic cells.
Biomass		Uses organic matter such as wood and crops. Energy is released by: • combustion • fermentation to produce alcohols which can be mixed with petrol • anaerobic digestion to produce biogas which can be burned.
Wind	 	Wind turbines convert the kinetic energy of the wind into electrical energy.
Wave		The potential energy of the difference in height between the crest and trough of a wave is converted into kinetic energy for turning a turbine to generate electricity.
Hydroelectric		When rain falls on high land the water has potential energy. As the water flows downhill, this is converted into kinetic energy which can be used to turn turbines to generate electricity. The photo shows the controversial Three Gorges Dam in China.
Tidal		The gravitational attraction of the Moon and Sun causes the tides to rise and fall. Water held behind a barrage at high tide can be allowed to run back into the sea as the tide falls, turning turbines as it goes.
Geothermal		Rocks deep underground contain elements that are radioactively decaying which heats rocks and turns underground water into steam which can turn turbines for electricity generation.

Although there are many differences between nuclear fuel, fossil fuels and renewable sources of energy, there are some common principles in how electricity is generated using them (see Diagram **G**).

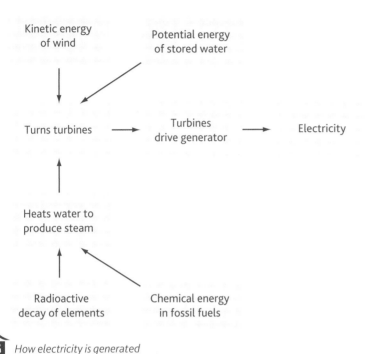

G *How electricity is generated*

Biofuels are a controversial source of renewable energy. The fuels are used up as they are burnt but they can still be described as renewable if new biofuel crops are quickly grown again. Several different types of biofuels have been developed: some of them are made from crops grown specially for the purpose while others are obtained from plant and animal waste products.

- Sugar (usually from tropical sugar cane) can be fermented to produce alcohol. This can be mixed with petrol and used as vehicle fuel.
- Oil crops (including oilseed rape, soya and palm oil) produce vegetable oil used in cooking but the oil can also be processed into biodiesel.
- Another type of biodiesel is made from waste cooking oil.
- Crops, including fast-growing varieties of willow, can be grown and burnt for electricity generation in thermal power stations.
- Animal and plant waste, including human sewage, can be fermented to produce biogas.

Some people argue that biofuels can be used sustainably because although they give off carbon dioxide when they are burnt this only puts back into the atmosphere carbon dioxide which has recently been taken out during photosynthesis. Biofuel technologies which use waste products also seem to be a good idea. On the other hand there are worries about the effects on the environment when land is cleared to grow biofuel crops and also that growing them may reduce the amount of land available to grow crops, making food more expensive.

Floating wind turbines

The government has teamed up with scientists and engineers from several countries to form The Energy Technologies Institute (ETI).

Their job? To solve the problem that, whilst the UK is very windy, some people do not like wind turbines – they think they are ugly and noisy (although perhaps not as ugly and noisy as a coal power station…).

ETI's proposed solution was to construct offshore wind farms – but it is difficult to build wind turbines in water that is more than 30 m deep. To solve this, the scientists are developing wind turbines that float!

Floating rigs are already commonly used to extract oil and gas and it is hoped that the international team will be able to design floating turbines that can be put far out to sea, silent and invisible to people living on land.

Environmental scientists@work

H *An offshore wind farm*

What are the advantages and disadvantages of various energy resources?

Environmental scientists consider the advantages and disadvantages of various energy resources before making conclusions and recommendations. Some of the questions that they ask about efficiency and environmental impact include:

- Is the enery supply predictable? I.e. what is the certainty that a source will deliver a particular amount at a particular time?
- Is the energy supply inermittent? I.e. does it stop and start?
- Does the energy resource result in harmful emissions to air or water?
- Does exploiting the resource mean that land or habitats are destroyed?
- What wastes are produced and in what quantity?
- Does exploiting the resource affect other important activities, for example, radar monitoring of aircraft or the migration of animals?

One difficulty is that different people have different priorities. While one person might believe that no new nuclear plants should be developed until safe radioactive waste disposal is organised, another would vote for a nuclear power station rather than have their favourite moorland landscape 'ruined' by wind turbines.

Group activity

Copy the table below. Working in small groups, discuss and 'score' each type of energy resource on the factors shown in the table. You can give any factor a score of 0 to 10 where 0 represents a huge disadvantage and 10 a huge advantage. So, for example, if you think that the production of radioactive waste is a huge disadvantage of nuclear power, you might score it 0 or 1. If you think that, on balance, the fact that nuclear power doesn't release huge volumes of greenhouse gases is a fairly big advantage you might score it 7, 8 or 9.

Once you've given every factor for each resource a score, add up the total score for that resource. Then compare your preferred energy resource with that of other groups! So which energy resource did you score the highest?

	Energy resource					
	Fossil fuels	Nuclear power	Biofuels	Tidal power	Solar power	Wind power
Predictability						
Intermittency						
Emissions to air and water						
Land loss through mining or quarrying						
Disturbance to sediment patterns/ water flow						
Production of hazardous waste						
Wildlife disruption						
Noise pollution/ radio disturbance						
Loss of landscape						
Total score						

Sitting higher tier

Nuclear fuel is said to be 'energy-dense'. This means that, compared to coal, oil or gas, it can release large amounts of energy from very small amounts of fuel.

In general, fossil fuels, nuclear fuel and biofuels are going to provide a more predictable or continuous supply of energy than solar, wind or tidal sources. Once 5 million tonnes of coal have been bought, it is known how much energy can be guaranteed to the country's consumers and so roughly how long it will last. However, there is no certainty that it will be sunny or windy.

On the other hand, we know that burning fossil fuels will release carbon dioxide and oxides of nitrogen that are powerful greenhouse gases. Wind farms, tidal power and solar power do not do this. Extraction of coal, in particular, will disrupt wildlife but then again, the Ministry of Defence claim that wind farms disrupt radar, potentially allowing enemy aircraft to get past our air defences.

The answer may well be to try to meet our energy requirements from a mix of most or all of the above energy resources!

Activity

2 Graph I shows how demand for electricity varies during a typical winter day in the UK.

a Suggest why the demand for electricity varies in this way.

b What problems might this cause if most of our electricity were to be produced by renewable technologies?

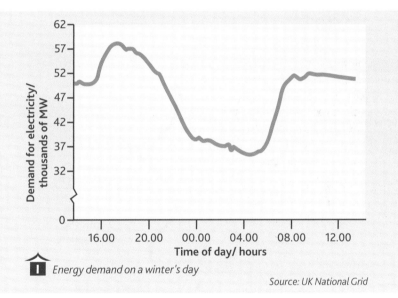

I *Energy demand on a winter's day*

Source: UK National Grid

Summary

Nuclear power stations split atoms of uranium and plutonium, releasing large amounts of energy which, just as in a coal-fired plant, is used to super-heat water to turn turbines which enables electricity generation.

Nuclear power stations produce small amounts of extremely dangerous wastes that have to be stored for thousands of years.

Renewable energy resources such as solar power and wind power are sustainable and non-polluting, whereas fossil fuels are a finite resource and are highly polluting.

The ultimate source of energy in many renewables is the Sun.

Each type of energy resource has its advantages and disadvantages. The best way forward may be to aim for an energy mix.

A3.1 Why is the greenhouse effect important for life on Earth?

■ What is the natural greenhouse effect?

Some people think that the greenhouse effect is something new and that it is altogether bad. In fact, the Earth's atmosphere creates a natural greenhouse effect which is vital in helping to keep the Earth warm enough to support life. Without this natural warming effect, the average temperature on Earth would be about –17 °C! Life as we know it would be impossible.

In this section you will learn:

about the importance of the natural greenhouse effect

about the main greenhouse gases

about the main processes, stores and sinks in the carbon cycle.

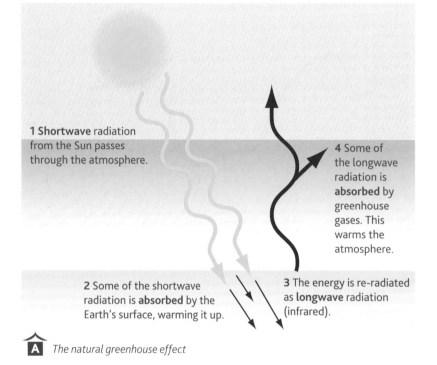

1 **Shortwave** radiation from the Sun passes through the atmosphere.

4 Some of the longwave radiation is **absorbed** by greenhouse gases. This warms the atmosphere.

2 Some of the shortwave radiation is **absorbed** by the Earth's surface, warming it up.

3 The energy is re-radiated as **longwave** radiation (infrared).

A *The natural greenhouse effect*

Key terms

Shortwave radiation: the radiation which comes from the Sun and warms the Earth's surface. This radiation is mainly visible light.

Longwave radiation: this is the radiation which is re-radiated from the Earth's surface. It is mainly infrared radiation.

AQA *Examiner's tip*

You need to learn how the greenhouse effect works. Candidates often get confused about which type of radiation (**shortwave** or **longwave**) comes from the Sun and which type is re-radiated by the Earth. They also lose marks by writing about radiation being reflected when they should be writing about it being absorbed and then re-radiated. Learn the diagram, including the labels.

What are the main greenhouse gases?

There are four main greenhouse gases: carbon dioxide, water vapour, methane and nitrous oxide (Table **B**). Each is created and added to the atmosphere in a different way.

B *Greenhouse gases*

Greenhouse gas	Natural sources
Carbon dioxide	Respiration of plants and animals
	Natural fires burning organic matter
Water vapour	Precipitation and evaporation
Methane	Bacteria breaking down organic matter anaerobically (without using oxygen)
Nitrous oxide	Bacteria breaking down organic matter

Water vapour is responsible for most of the natural greenhouse effect and although there are only tiny amounts of methane and nitrous oxide in the atmosphere, they are both more powerful greenhouse gases than carbon dioxide.

What are the main processes in the carbon cycle?

The amount of carbon dioxide in the atmosphere is regulated (controlled) by the processes of the carbon cycle (Diagram **C**). Understanding the main processes in the carbon cycle will help you to understand the greenhouse effect debate more clearly.

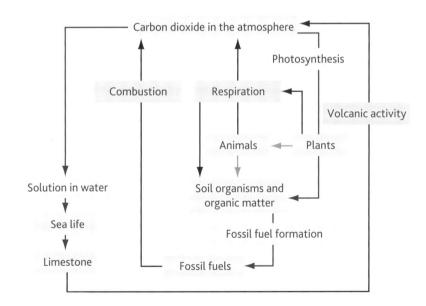

Processes which add carbon dioxide to the atmosphere

Processes which remove carbon dioxide from the atmosphere

Stores of carbon

C *The carbon cycle*

Activity

1 Use the internet or books to find out how much of each natural greenhouse gas there is in the atmosphere.

AQA *Examiner's tip*

You will never be asked to draw your own diagram of the carbon cycle in an exam question, but you could easily be given one and asked questions about it or asked to add missing labels. Be prepared for different styles of diagram (square boxes or ovals, straight arrows or curved ones, words or pictures, with numerical values or without).

There are three major natural processes which remove carbon dioxide from the atmosphere and another three which add carbon dioxide to the atmosphere:

D

Taking carbon dioxide out of the atmosphere	Adding carbon dioxide to the atmosphere
Photosynthesis: Plants use carbon dioxide in the process of making food. The carbon dioxide is incorporated into living plants and can be passed on through the food chain to animals.	**Respiration**: All plants and animals and many microorganisms obtain energy from their food by aerobic respiration. This returns carbon dioxide to the atmosphere.
Fossil fuel formation: Most of the carbon dioxide removed during photosynthesis is returned to the atmosphere quite quickly by respiration, but over millions of years the remains of huge quantities of plants and animals have been buried beneath layers of sediment and are stored as fossil fuels.	**Combustion**: Carbon dioxide is formed when any substance containing carbon is burnt in air. This may not be a problem when the substance being burnt is organic matter which has been formed recently (e.g. wood) because the burning process returns carbon dioxide to the atmosphere which has recently been removed by photosynthesis.
Solution in water: Carbon dioxide dissolves in water and huge amounts are stored in the oceans. Some of the dissolved carbon dioxide is used by sea life and can be incorporated into limestone, removing it from circulation in the carbon cycle.	**Volcanic eruptions**: These give off huge amounts of carbon dioxide.

A carbon store is a place in the environment where carbon is found. Carbon stores include the atmosphere (where the carbon is in the form of carbon dioxide), the bodies of plants and animals (where it exists as glucose, starch and other compounds), soil organic matter and limestone rock (where it is in the form of the mineral calcium carbonate).

A carbon sink is a carbon store which, over a long period of time, takes in more carbon dioxide from the atmosphere than it gives out. Examples include growing forests, peat bogs and the seas and oceans.

Key terms

Photosynthesis: the process by which plants (and some micro-organisms) make food using carbon dioxide, water and light energy.

Respiration: the process by which organisms break down their food to release energy. Respiration can be aerobic (using oxygen) or anaerobic (happening without oxygen). Carbon dioxide is released by this process.

Environmental scientists@work

Studying the global carbon cycle

Scientists from the National Oceanic and Atmospheric Administration (NOAA), in the United States, are working with hundreds of scientists from around the world studying the global carbon cycle.

Many scientists are based on research vessels in the oceans. By measuring how carbon dioxide concentrations in the world's oceans are changing, they hope to be able to predict what effect rising temperatures will have on the major carbon stores, such as the oceans and the atmosphere.

Activity

2 a In pairs, each draw either a diagram showing the greenhouse effect or a diagram showing the carbon cycle but leave out half of the labels. (Your diagram can be as simple or as complex as time allows and it is up to you how many illustrations you use and the style of the arrows, boxes for labels, and so on.)

   b When you have finished (but still with half the labels missing) swap your diagram with your partner. Now complete your partner's diagram by adding the missing labels.

Summary

Gases in the Earth's atmosphere help to regulate the temperature through the greenhouse effect.

Greenhouse gases allow shortwave radiation from the Sun to pass through but trap some of the out-going longwave radiation, increasing the temperature of the atmosphere.

A3.2 How may human activities change the climate?

The greenhouse effect is a natural process that is essential for life on Earth. Without it, average temperatures would be below freezing in many places. The problem is that human activities are increasing the amout of greenhouse gases and these are absorbing more longwave radiation, heating the lower atmosphere.

The main greenhouse gases that are responsible for global climate change are carbon dioxide, methane, nitrous oxide and CFCs (chlorofluorocarbons). Diagram **A** shows how the concentrations of carbon dioxide, methane and nitrous oxide have increased since the Industrial Revolution.

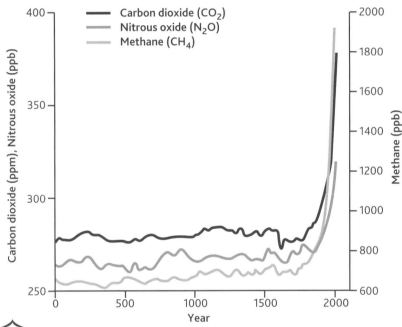

A *Concentrations of the main greenhouse gases*
Source: IPCC, Fourth Assessment Report, 2007

Activity

1   Which of these three greenhouse gases (carbon dioxide, methane and nitrous oxide) is at the highest concentration in the atmosphere in the year 2000?

You need to look closely at the units for these three gases. The units for carbon dioxide are parts per million (ppm), but the units for methane and nitrous oxide are parts per billion (ppb). You can see that in 2000, the concentration of nitrous oxide (the green line) was about 1250 ppb. In other words, in a sample of air taken in the year 2000, we would find 1250 molecules of nitrous oxide for every billion molecules of air.

All three of these gases have been rapidly increasing in the atmosphere since about 1750. Humans are responsible!

Photosynthesis is the main process that removes carbon dioxide from the atmosphere. Humans have cleared millions of hectares of forest (**deforestation**) to make way for agriculture, cities and reservoirs, and so on. So we have reduced enormously the amount of vegetation that is capable of removing carbon dioxide from the atmosphere through

Key terms

Deforestation: the felling of forests.

photosynthesis. Worse still, having chopped down the forests, we usually burn the wood, releasing even more carbon dioxide.

As human population has increased, so too has our need for energy – for transport, industrial processes and heating (Section A2.1).

Most of this energy has been obtained by burning fossil fuels – coal, oil and gas. All fossil fuels contain carbon – so burning (oxidising) them releases carbon dioxide.

Atmospheric scientists now estimate that carbon dioxide levels are the highest they have been for at least 420 000 years and probably the highest they have been for 20 million years!

Environmental scientists@work

Ice bubbles

Scientists in Greenland and Antarctica have been extracting huge ice cores to investigate what the climate was like tens of thousands of years ago. Snow contains tiny bubbles of air. These bubbles remain even when the snow becomes compacted into ice. Snow that fell in Greenland 1500 years ago is now ice, buried under 30 m of ice and snow that has formed on top of it. The bubbles in that 1500 year-old snow are an accurate reflection of what the atmosphere was like when it fell. So the scientists can measure the amount of carbon dioxide in the bubbles and this tells them how much carbon dioxide was in the air then. They know that, the more carbon dioxide is in the air, the warmer the atmosphere. So the ice core bubbles are like a ancient thermometer, telling us the temperature of the atmosphere over the last 400 000 years!

B *A scientist examining an ice core*

More humans have also meant more livestock. Unfortunately, all **ruminants** such as cows, sheep and goats release methane when they digest cellulose from plants. Methane is 23 times more powerful than carbon dioxide at increasing the temperature of the atmosphere. Worldwide, hundreds of millions of people depend on rice as their staple food. Most rice is grown in paddies – waterlogged fields. The anaerobic conditions in the soil provide perfect conditions for bacteria to breakdown organic matter, releasing methane.

As countries become richer and more developed, they tend to eat more meat. This is bad news on two counts. More forests will be chopped down so less carbon dioxide is absorbed and the wood burned to make way for pasture releases more carbon dioxide. Also more cattle being reared for food will mean more methane is released from anaerobic digestion.

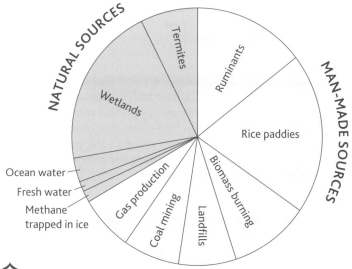

C *Natural and man-made sources of methane*

Imagine too just how much waste food and other organic matter humans have dumped or put into landfill sites over the past 300 years. When this decomposes in conditions where there is little oxygen (anaerobic), methane is released.

Burning fossil fuels in vehicles and power stations releases nitrous oxide, another powerful greenhouse gas. Agriculture is also a big artificial source of this gas. Worldwide, farmers apply millions of tonnes of nitrate fertilisers to help their crops grow. Bacteria in the soil convert some of these nitrates into nitrous oxide gas before the roots of the plants can absorb them. So the increased use of nitrogen fertilisers has contributed to rapidly increasing levels of this gas in the atmosphere.

Chlorofluorocarbons (CFCs), a group of gases that contain the elements chlorine, fluorine and carbon, are also important greenhouse gases. But unlike carbon dioxide, methane and nitrous oxide, all of which are naturally present in the atmosphere, CFCs are totally artificial. An American engineer invented them in 1928 and, over the next 60 years, they were used all over the world as:

- coolants in refrigerators and air conditioning units
- propellants in aerosol cans
- solvents for cleaning circuit boards.

Once released into the atmosphere, they stay there for 20–100 years. Unfortunately, they are very powerful greenhouse gases. CFC use has been banned in all developed countries and the concentration of many CFCs is now falling rapidly – a success story!

Methane to markets

Scientists working for the United Nations Environment Programme (UNEP) are investigating how methane from decomposing animal wastes (manure and urine) can be collected and used as a fuel to generate heat or electricity. They estimate that, globally, the anaerobic decomposition of animal wastes releases millions of tonnes of methane and in China, 10 per cent of all methane comes from this source.

D *Sources of greenhouse gases*

Greenhouse gas	Sources
Carbon dioxide	Burning fossil fuels for domestic heating and cooking, industry and transport
	Deforestation
Methane	Livestock farming to supply consumers with meat, milk and other dairy products
	Rice paddyfields
	Landfill sites
Nitrous oxide	Burning fossil fuels for domestic heating and cooking, industry and transport
	Using nitrate fertilisers to grow crops such as wheat for production of cereals and bread
CFCs	Refrigerators, aerosol cans and solvents

Summary

Deforestation reduces the amount of vegetation that is able to remove carbon dioxide from the atmosphere by photosynthesis.

Burning felled trees releases yet more carbon dioxide.

All fossil fuels contain carbon, so burning them releases carbon dioxide.

The main man-made sources of methane are rice-growing, ruminant digestion, and biomass burning.

The main sources of nitrous oxide are through the application of nitrate fertilisers and the burning of fossil fuels.

CFCs are man-made greenhouse gases that were widely used in refrigerators and as propellants in aerosol cans. Their use has been banned in developed countries.

2 In a table, make a quick list of everything you did yesterday. Include in your list the things that used energy or water and everything you ate. The table below gives you some examples of the kind of things you might include. Then, use Table **D** to fill in the right-hand column of your table identifying which greenhouse gases your activities released.

What I did yesterday	Process involved	Greenhouse gases released
Woke up when alarm clock went off	Uses electricity	Carbon dioxide
Had shower	Uses electricity to heat water	Carbon dioxide
Had toast	Toaster uses electricity	Carbon dioxide
Had glass of milk	Milk from cow	Cow produces methane

You may have realized that even everyday actions such as drinking milk or eating toast will have resulted in more greenhouse gases being released. These greenhouse gases absorb more of the longwave radiation that is emitted from the surface of the Earth, adding to the overall warming of the planet.

3 Graph **E** shows how the amount of carbon dioxide in the atmosphere has changed over the past 1000 years. Scientists obtained the data to draw this graph from ice cores in Greenland.

a Explain how ice cores can be used to work out how much carbon dioxide was in the atmosphere 1000 years ago.

b Describe the trend shown in Graph **E**.

c Suggest two ways in which human activity has been responsible for the trend shown.

d What is the consequence of this trend for Earth's atmospheric temperature?

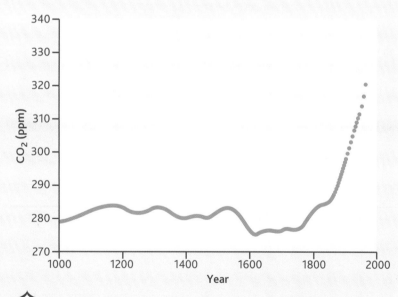

E *Levels of carbon dioxide in the atmosphere*

Source: CSIRO Atmospheric Research

A3.3   What are the potential effects of global climate change?

How is climate likely to change?

Environmental scientists are now certain that the average surface temperature of Earth has increased by about 0.7 °C over the 20th century. That's the greatest increase of any century during the past 1000 years. They are also certain that this is a result of human activity, including mine and yours!

Most scientists expect average temperatures to go up even further but it is difficult to predict by how much. This is because the Earth's climate is influenced by many complex processes that interact with each other. As the Earth gets hotter, some processes are triggered that make it even hotter still. But other processes may be triggered that help to cool it back down. Trying to work out what the overall effect will be requires computer modeling and different computer models show different amounts of warming.

Diagram **A** shows three estimates of temperature increases this century.

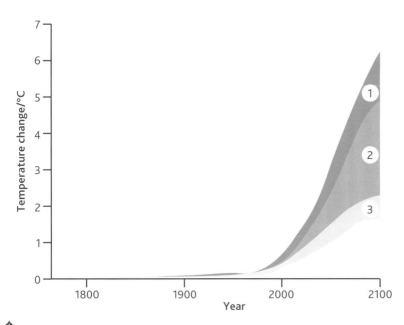

A   *Three estimates of temperature change in the 21st century*

Source: STERN REVIEW: The Economics of Climate Change, HM Treasury
www.hm-treasury.gov.uk/stern_review_report.htm

In this section you will learn:

about potential changes to the Earth's climate caused by human activities

how climate change may affect sea levels, food production and wildlife

about some of the changes in climate which happened before human activities became important.

How science works

When scientists do investigations using enzymes in test tubes in the laboratory, they can control all the other variables that might affect the result. They can predict with confidence what result they are going to get. But, in stimulating global climate change, humans are conducting an investigation not in a test tube, or a lab, or even a country, but across the entire planet. The variables are huge and unpredictable – ocean temperatures, plant growth, decomposition rates, cloud formations – all of these could influence the final temperature of the planet. This is why there is such a big difference between the minimum and maximum temperature change in Diagram **A**.

Besides being warmer, environmental scientists believe that the climate will also become more extreme. Storms, floods and droughts will become more common or more intense in many areas.

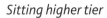

Warmer and cooler

Scientists agree that some areas of the world are going to get warmer, while others will, in fact, become cooler. But predicting which of these will happen in particular areas is tricky. Heat is moved around the planet via ocean currents and high altitude winds. If these alter as a result of the warming that we have caused, then large areas of the planet will change temperature. However, the consequences of this may be very different in different continents.

For example, the average temperature in some parts of Africa is expected to increase by 1–2 °C. Temperatures are also expected to increase in the Himalayas.

On the other hand, countries such as the UK might even end up cooler! This is because today ocean currents drawn from the tropics warm the UK, along with other countries in Western Europe. But in the future, melting glaciers and increased rainfall may result in this heat pump slowing down or even stopping. This could cool the whole North Atlantic region.

■ How may climate change affect conditions on Earth?

Environmental scientists use a wide range of techniques to predict the effects of human activities on climate change (Table **B**).

B

Technique	What it can tell us
Using satellites and thermal imaging techniques	Which parts of the world's oceans are warming up and how much sea levels are rising
Extracting 3 km cylinders of ice from Antarctica	What the atmosphere was like over the past 400 000 years
Trapping insects across Europe	Whether insect pests are colonising areas further north as these warm up
Growing crops in greenhouses with higher concentrations of carbon dioxide	Whether crops grow more quickly or more slowly? After all, they need carbon dioxide to photosynthesise
Sticking poles into glaciers	Whether the glacier is getting bigger (the poles are covered in ice) or whether it is getting smaller (the poles fall out)

Changing rainfall patterns

One of the most serious consequences of increasing temperatures is that there will be changes in the amount, timing and distribution of precipitation. The combination of increasing temperatures and increasing human population will result in more people and wildlife facing severe water shortages. One scientific study reported that a temperature rise of 2 °C would result in 1 to 4 billion people in Africa, the Middle East, Southern Europe, and parts of South and Central America facing serious water shortages.

At the same time, between 1 and 5 billion people living in South and East Asia may receive more water. The problem here is that most of this extra rainfall will occur in the wet season. This will cause flooding unless more reservoirs are built to store it.

Coastal erosion

For millions of people, increasing temperatures will bring rising sea levels, more coastal flooding and **coastal erosion**. This will threaten people's homes and property, agricultural land and wildlife habitats.

Sea levels will rise as a result of two processes:

1 Land glaciers will melt faster, adding more water to the oceans
2 The ocean temperature will increase and the water will expand thermally

In fact, both of these events are already happening.

The Greenland ice cap covers an area of 1.75 million km². It is a huge store of frozen fresh water on land. Each year, part of the ice cap melts, before refreezing again later in the year. But as the climate warms, the size of the area melting has been increasing – and the area that refreezes later is getting smaller (see Diagram **D**). The pattern of melting closely matches the pattern of increasing global average temperatures.

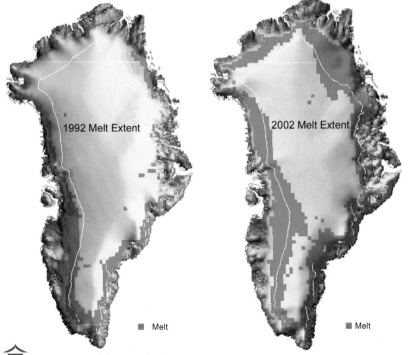

1992 Melt Extent   2002 Melt Extent

■ Melt   ■ Melt

D *Glacier melt of the Greenland ice cap*

C *Coastal erosion is putting homes at risk*

Activity

1 Describe the differences in the amount and distribution of ice melt in Greenland in the two years shown in Diagram **D**.

Georg Kaser is an ice scientist (glaciologist) at the University of Innsbruck, Austria. His team used stakes and holes drilled into 300 land glaciers to record the change in their mass over the past 70 years. Their research has shown that 99.99 per cent of all glaciers are now shrinking.

The glaciers are going to melt and melt until they are all gone. There are not any glaciers getting bigger any more.

E   *Retreat of the Jakobshavn Isbrae glacier in Greenland*

Melting land glaciers have contributed to sea level rise but this isn't the only problem! Millions of people rely on the annual glacier melt for their water for drinking, cleaning, cooking and irrigation of their crops. For example, annual meltwater from glaciers in the Himalayas supplies seven of Asia's biggest rivers, including 70 per cent of the summer flow in the Ganges, which provides water to 500 million people in India. If the glaciers disappear, so does their water supply.

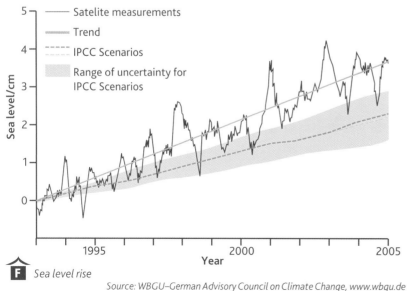

F   *Sea level rise*

Source: WBGU–German Advisory Council on Climate Change, www.wbgu.de

Activity

2   Use the internet or your local library to identify which of the world's major cities are at severe risk of flooding by the expected increase in sea levels.

Hint: There are 22 of them!

As sea levels rise, coastal flooding will increase. Unfortunately, coastal areas are often densely populated. More than 200 million people live in coastal floodplains and 2 million km² of land is less than 1 m above sea level. It seems very likely that, in your lifetime, millions of people, perhaps hundred of millions, will be forced to move regions or even countries to escape the floods. They will become **climate refugees**.

Increasing global temperatures will affect food supplies as well as water supplies. At first glance, a warmer world looks like good news for agriculture. Plants produce food by photosynthesis and photosynthesis speeds up as temperature increases. So, increasing temperatures means more food!

Unfortunately, it's not as simple as this. Crop growth is influenced by temperature, but also by water availability and, as we have seen, water may become a scarce resource over large areas of the planet. Rainfall may become less reliable and areas may become drier or wetter than they are today. Plant scientists predict that even small increases in temperature will reduce crop yields in tropical areas, where malnutrition already kills 2 million people every year.

However, small increases in average temperature in mid to high latitudes (Europe, US, Siberia, Australia and some parts of China) may increase crop growth by increasing the length of the growing season. But, if the temperature increase exceeds 3 °C, then yields are predicted to fall as a result of water shortages.

Key terms
Climate refugees: people who are forced to flee their regions or countries because of flooding or other environmental problems caused by climate change.

Activity

3   Graph **G** shows two estimates of the number of extra people at risk of hunger as global temperature increases.

Suggest three reasons why increasing temperatures may result in more people suffering hunger.

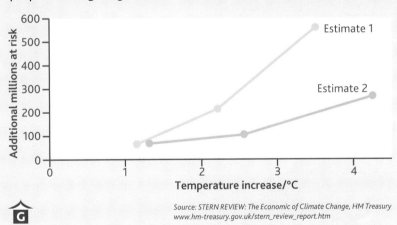

Source: STERN REVIEW: The Economic of Climate Change, HM Treasury
www.hm-treasury.gov.uk/stern_review_report.htm

G

Although humans are responsible for climate change, it is likely that every other species of plant and animal will be affected by it. In biological communities species interact in complex ways. These interactions have evolved over thousands of years. Now, species face sudden and dramatic changes in their environment.

In 2002, the Intergovernmental Panel on Climate Change (IPCC) reported that, of the more than 500 birds, amphibians, plants and other organisms studied, 80 per cent had changed the timing of reproduction or migration, length of growing season, population size or population distribution in ways that might be expected from warming temperatures.

Climate change may happen too quickly for many species to adapt. The Amazon rainforest contains more species than anywhere else on Earth, but if the entire region receives less rainfall, then the rainforest will not survive. The resulting loss of biodiversity would be a catastrophe. Similarly, scientists are worried that some of the very places that environmental scientists and governments have created to try to conserve wildlife – African National Parks, for example, will become too dry to support their wildlife.

Pied flycatchers

Biologists working at the National Museum of Science in Madrid, Spain have spent 20 years studying pied flycatchers.

Pied flycatchers spend the summer in Spain and then fly off to west Africa for some winter sun! In 1980, these birds would arrive back in Spain in April. The biggest number of birds would arrive on 25 April. They would breed and their eggs would hatch in June, with the biggest number of eggs hatching on 3 June. This was perfect timing because 3 June was also the day that the biggest numbers of tasty caterpillars appeared on oak leaves. The flycatcher chicks had plenty of food.

Twenty years later, in 2000, climate change has altered this relationship. The flycatchers are still arriving back in Spain on 25 April. But the oak trees and caterpillars are now out-of-step with the birds. The warmer temperatures have meant that oak leaves appear earlier than they used to. The caterpillars have responded by appearing earlier to eat these leaves. Even though the flycatcher's eggs are hatching earlier than they used to (25 May), this is 10 days after most of the caterpillars have appeared (15 May). Fewer flycatcher chicks are surviving.

H *A pied flycatcher*

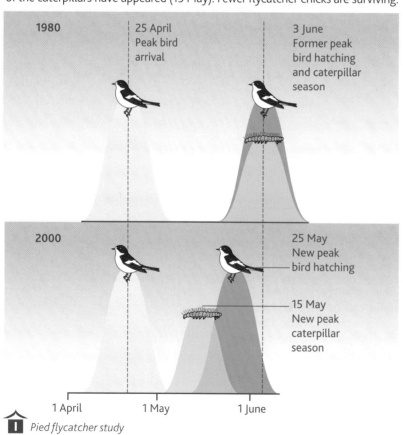

1980

25 April
Peak bird arrival

3 June
Former peak bird hatching and caterpillar season

2000

25 May
New peak bird hatching

15 May
New peak caterpillar season

1 April   1 May   1 June

I *Pied flycatcher study*

Activity

4 Use the information given in the Environmental scientists@work box on page 74 to complete the table.

	1980	2000
Day when most flycatchers arrive back in Spain		
Day when most flycatcher eggs hatch		
Day when most caterpillars hatch		

There is growing evidence that species of plants, insects, fish and birds are colonising areas further north as these areas warm up. This raises a lot of questions for scientists:

- Will they survive the journey north?
- How will they adapt to their new environment?
- How will the species that currently live there respond?
- Will the newcomers include disease-spreading organisms such as mosquitoes or viruses that affect livestock, e.g. Bluetongue?

This is a good time to be a scientist, there is a lot to discover!

Activity

5 Scientists predict that many species of plants and animals will move northwards as global temperatures increase. Suggest problems that this may cause for:

  a farmers

  b wildlife that currently lives in these northern habitats.

■ How has the Earth's climate changed over geological time?

Imagine that you are the new Dr Who. Your new assistant wants to go back 3 million years to see what the weather and locals are like. What would you find? Well, large areas of the planet would have been covered with ice (Map J). In what we now call Africa, the first humans had just evolved.

This was the beginning of a series of Ice Ages.

K *Australopithecines – one of our ancestors*

J *The extent of ice sheets in the last Ice Age (white regions)*

Diagram **L** shows that the Earth has gone through a natural cycle of temperature extremes – very cold ice ages followed by periods of much higher temperatures.

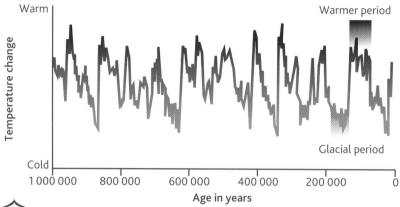

L Glacial and warmer periods

So climate change is normal and agriculture, wild species and ecosystems have adapted to climate change many times in the past. The bare soils that were left after an Ice Age would, over the next 2000–5000 years, develop into forest. Animal species that had become extinct during the freeze would be replaced by species from places further south that had escaped the ice. Plant species would survive by dispersing their seed far and wide.

All Ice Ages have been ended by periods of global warming. Indeed, the global warming which ended the last Ice Age was much greater than the current global warming predictions. However, all past Ice Ages have been ended by natural events. The danger is that the warming in the 20th and 21st century:

- is entirely artificial and therefore a disruption to the natural cycle
- will happen so fast that wildlife will not have time to adapt or migrate
- will cause large scale species extinction
- will cause devastation to human populations living on the coastlines
- will make it difficult for humans to be able to grow sufficient food.

Sitting higher tier

Heat and water stress

Millions of people, especially the elderly and those with heart problems are expected to face greater health threats in a warmer world. Perhaps the biggest threat is heat stroke. The heat wave in France in August 2003 caused 14 800 extra deaths over just 20 days! Educating people about how to avoid overheating will cost millions of pounds.

Plants face a slightly different problem. In order to carry out photosynthesis, plants need to absorb carbon dioxide from the atmosphere. They do this through microscopic holes in their leaves called stomata. But whilst stomata are open, water vapour can escape out of the plant. As temperatures rise, the amount of water lost in this way will increase. This water must be replaced to prevent wilting – but higher temperatures will mean drier soils. This water stress is expected to cause local extinction of some plant species.

Activity

6   Increasing concentrations of greenhouse gases such as carbon dioxide and methane are contributing to global climate change. Diagram **M** shows what effect this might have on an elephant wildlife reserve in Kenya.

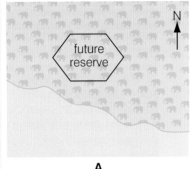

A
Before human settlement

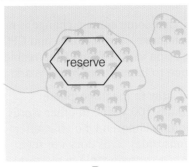

B
After human settlement

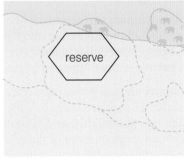

C
After climatic warming

Key

species distribution

grassland

desert

a   What effect did human habitation have on the distribution of elephants?

b   What effect is climate change expected to have on the distribution of elephants?

c   What problems might this cause?

Source: AQA, 2000

Summary

Global climate change will involve an increase in global temperature.

Intense storms, flooding and coastal erosion will become more common, but so will droughts.

Millions of people may face even more serious food or water shortages.

The speed of climate change may be too fast for some plant and animal species to adapt. Many are expected to become extinct.

Climate change is a natural process involving cycles of glacial and warmer periods. Many scientists believe that human activity is disrupting this natural cycle by causing very rapid warming.

A3.4 Can global climate change be stopped?

Why should we think about our carbon footprint?

Most environmental scientists believe that some climate change is now inevitable. So much carbon dioxide, methane, nitrous oxide and CFCs has been emitted that, even if the emission stopped now (impossible!), the Earth's temperature would continue to increase for many years.

Most greenhouse gases, once released, stay in the atmosphere absorbing longwave radiation, for around 100 years. In other words, it will be your children and your children's children who will suffer the worst consequences of the emissions today. This does not seem fair. Neither is it fair that, although it is wealthy people in western countries who are responsible for most emissions, it is the poorest people in LEDCs who are going to suffer the worst consequences of global climate change.

However, it is not all bad news. If we can reduce emissions of greenhouse gases now and in the future, then the worst consequences of climate change can be avoided. This will involve individuals, like me and you, industry and governments reducing their **carbon footprint**. The carbon footprint is defined as the environmental impact of the total amount of carbon dioxide and other greenhouse gases emitted over the full life cycle of the use of a product, service or event by individuals, specific activities or areas. So every time we buy a pair of trainers (a product) or boil the kettle (provision of electrical energy) or go to a concert (an event) we add to our carbon footprint.

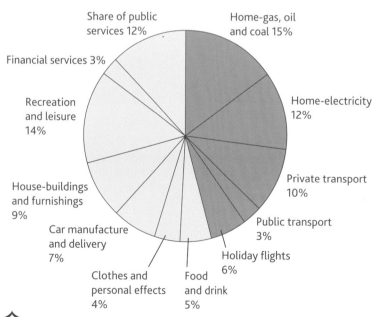

Share of public services 12%
Home-gas, oil and coal 15%
Financial services 3%
Home-electricity 12%
Recreation and leisure 14%
Private transport 10%
House-buildings and furnishings 9%
Public transport 3%
Car manufacture and delivery 7%
Holiday flights 6%
Clothes and personal effects 4%
Food and drink 5%

A *A typical person's carbon footprint*

Source: www.carbonfootprint.com

In this section you will learn:

about carbon footprints

about methods of reducing carbon dioxide emissions

how the carbon cycle can help us to understand and evaluate possible methods of reducing the carbon dioxide concentration of the atmosphere

about the difficulties in reducing our carbon footprint

about the Montreal Protocol as an example of a pollution control agreement which seems to be working.

Environmental scientists@work

Become a carbon footprint consultant!

Engineer John Buckley and Physicist Wendy Buckley have set up their own company – Carbon Footprint Ltd – to advise councils and businesses on ways in which they can reduce their carbon footprint, save money and meet changing legal requirements.

It's an exciting job. On a typical day, John and Wendy might be advising a council on ways to reduce carbon emissions from their town hall and calculating how much CO_2 is emitted during the production, use and disposal of a company's new product.

'We have to learn fast and deliver real savings to our customers. No two days are the same and it's great to be running a company that, in a small way, is helping safeguard the planet,' said John.

Find out more at **www.carbonfootprint.com**

A person's carbon footprint is made up of direct emissions of CO_2 from the burning of fossil fuels (for example, heating your house, cooking on a gas cooker, being driven to school) which are shown in green on the pie chart, and the 'hidden' CO_2 emissions from the whole lifecycle of products we buy and use. These are shown in yellow on the pie chart. We have direct control over the green elements and, because different versions of a particular product will have different carbon footprints, we can reduce our footprints by making informed choices!

How can carbon dioxide emissions be reduced?

Governments can reduce their country's carbon footprints by reducing their emissions of carbon dioxide. To do this, they need data collected by pollution scientists showing where the emissions are coming from.

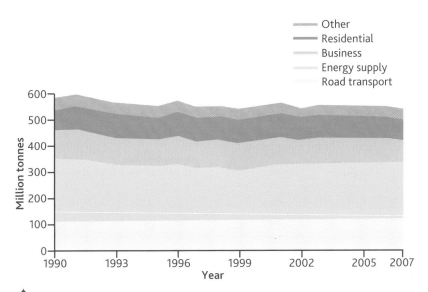

B *Carbon dioxide emissions by sector*

Source: Defra © Crown copyright

In Graph **B**, the mass of carbon dioxide released from each sector is shown.

The biggest four sectors in the graph are energy supply, road transport, residential and business. So these are the priority sectors for governments to consider. Let's look at each of these in turn.

Energy supply

Imagine that you are the government minister responsible for cutting the UK's carbon footprint by 2020. You know that we get our energy from fossil fuels, nuclear power and renewables. Which sources of energy would you increase and which would you decrease?

To cut carbon dioxide emissions it might be sensible to reduce the consumption of coal, oil and gas – the fossil fuels – because burning any fossil fuel will release carbon dioxide. Nuclear power stations and renewable energy sources such as wind, solar and tidal do not emit carbon dioxide when in use, so if more of them were used and less fossil fuels, the UK's carbon footprint would be reduced.

Activity

1 **a** Calculate your or your family's carbon footprint using the government's footprint calculator found at: www.direct.gov.uk/actonCO2.

   b Use Pie chart **A** of a typical person's carbon footprint to suggest why fitting draft excluders to the bottom of doors might reduce a person's carbon footprint.

   c The pie chart shows that the use of gas, oil, coal and electricity make up more than 25 per cent of a person's carbon footprint. Apart from fitting draught excluders, suggest four other ways in which this could be reduced.

Activity

2 Take a look at Graph **B**.

   a Which sector has released the most carbon dioxide each year?

   b Which sector has produced just over 100 million tonnes of carbon dioxide each year since 1990?

   c In 2007, the residential sector (houses) released approximately what percentage of total carbon dioxide emissions?

   A 25%   B 70%
   C 14%   D 40%

However, there is a way of burning fossil fuels that does not add to the carbon footprint. This is called **carbon capture and storage** (see Diagram **C**). It involves capturing the carbon dioxide gas before it escapes out of the power station chimney, cooling and compressing it, and then storing it in porous rocks underground or under the seabed in disused oil and gas fields.

There are no power stations in the UK that can do this yet but, as Energy Minister, you might decide to invest millions of pounds into carbon capture and storage research because if it worked, you could then use fossil fuels at the same time as developing renewable sources of energy. Many other countries that depend heavily on fossil fuels would also be interested in buying this new technology from the UK, so this might be a good way of supplying the country's energy needs and generating jobs!

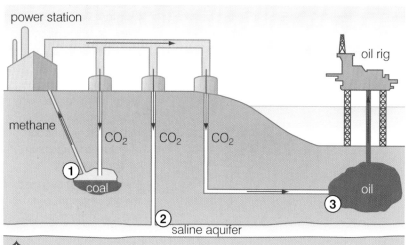

C *Carbon capture and storage*

Many scientists support the idea of **carbon taxes** as a way of reducing emissions from power stations, businesses and industry. In simple terms, the more carbon dioxide a power station, for example, emitted, the more tax it would pay. This tax could be collected through the existing tax system and the monies could then be used to help develop new, cleaner technology.

Transport emissions

Emissions of carbon dioxide from road transport are increasing in the UK and worldwide. Emissions could be decreased by increasing the price of fuel or by subsidising the cost of vehicles that run on 'greener' fuels or, perhaps in the future, hydrogen, which only produces water when it is burned.

D *Car emissions*

Activity

Diagram **E** compares our energy sources in 1980 and 2007.

3 Jot down the main changes in our energy sources between 1980 and 2007.

You probably noted the following:

- Oil consumption went down.
- Gas consumption more than doubled.
- Coal consumption decreased.
- The contribution of nuclear energy increased.
- Renewables and wastes started to contribute to our energy supplies.

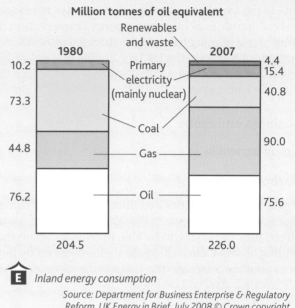

Million tonnes of oil equivalent

1980

Renewables and waste
Primary electricity (mainly nuclear)
Coal
Gas
Oil

10.2
73.3
44.8
76.2

204.5

2007

4.4
15.4
40.8
90.0
75.6

226.0

E Inland energy consumption

Source: Department for Business Enterprise & Regulatory Reform, UK Energy in Brief, July 2008 © Crown copyright

Sitting higher tier

Biofuels for transport are controversial

Biofuels are produced from crops such as cereals, oilseed rape and sugar beet. They can be used in cars, vans, buses and lorries. Their supporters claim that they have two big advantages over fossil fuels like diesel and petrol:

- They are sustainable, because the crops can continue to be grown, whereas all fossil fuels are finite and will run out.
- They are **carbon neutral**. Although carbon dioxide is produced when they are burned in engines, the same volume of carbon dioxide was absorbed by the crops during their growth. So, overall, biofuels result in zero net release of carbon dioxide.

Other scientists are very worried about biofuels and point out that some countries, such as Brazil, have destroyed millions of hectares of forest to grow biofuel crops.

Activity

4 Use the internet to identify reasons why biofuels may not, in practice, be carbon neutral.

Cheap air flights have encouraged millions more people to take holidays abroad. A return flight from London to Alicante in Spain (1763 miles) releases 0.4 tonnes of carbon dioxide. A growing number of companies now allow air travellers to **offset** these emissions. This involves paying the company to plant trees that will then absorb the 0.4 tonnes of carbon dioxide in photosynthesis. This way, the **net** effect of the flight is zero tonnes of carbon dioxide.

Key terms

Sitting higher tier

Carbon neutral: an energy source, e.g. sugar beet, that, when burned, releases no net CO_2. The amount of CO_2 released equals that which was absorbed by the plant in photosynthesis.

Carbon offsetting: paying for trees to be planted to absorb CO_2 to make up for that which was released by a person's activity, e.g. flying abroad.

F A biofuel pump

Residential emissions

One of the simplest and most effective ways to reduce emissions of carbon dioxide is to introduce **energy conservation** measures in the home. New housing has to meet strict energy conservation targets but millions of homes in the UK lack double glazing, proper loft insulation or cavity wall insulation, all of which would reduce the amount of valuable heat energy that quickly escapes to the outside.

Business emissions

Sitting higher tier

Carbon licences

Power stations, factories and other industrial or commercial businesses that release a lot of carbon dioxide can purchase a **carbon licence**. In effect, they are paying to be able to release carbon dioxide. Carbon trading allows them to increase their emissions by buying a licence from another company that is not using its quota. If the licensed quota is exceeded, they will be fined.

■ How policies to reduce carbon dioxide in the atmosphere can be evaluated

Many scientists have suggested ways of reducing the amount of carbon dioxide in the atmosphere. Some are relatively cheap and technically quite simple, others are extremely expensive and complex. The carbon cycle can be used to evaluate these policies.

Key terms

Energy Conservation: the practice of decreasing the amount of energy used in the home. This is often by reducing heat loss and using more efficient appliances.

Sitting higher tier

Carbon licence: bought by companies who pay to emit a certain amount of carbon dioxide.

Activity

5   Briefly describe three ways of reducing the concentration of carbon dioxide in the atmosphere.

Carbon dioxide in the atmosphere

Photosynthesis

Combustion   Respiration

Volcanic activity

Animals ← Plants

Solution in water

Soil organisms and organic matter

Sea life

Fossil fuel formation

Limestone   Fossil fuels

Processes which add carbon dioxide to the atmosphere

Processes which remove carbon dioxide from the atmosphere

Stores of carbon

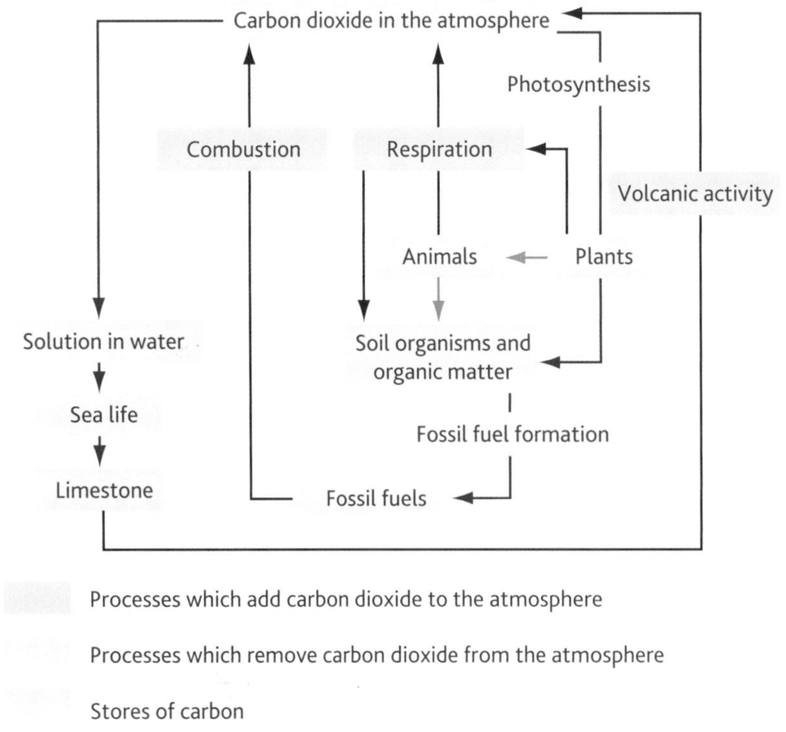

G *The carbon cycle*

Why will it be difficult to reduce the global carbon footprint?

Most people agree that the worst extremes of global climate change must be prevented. But not everyone!

A few scientists believe that there is not enough evidence that climate change is caused by human activities. They argue that the increasing average global temperature could still be part of the natural cycle. If they are correct, spending billions to reduce emissions of carbon dioxide would be a huge waste of time, effort and money.

Individuals are being urged to do their bit by turning lights off when they leave a room, walking to school instead of driving and wearing thick jumpers instead of turning the thermostat up, and so on. But surveys have shown that many members of the public are confused about climate change.

Are the media confusing the public?

Over the past 10 years, different parts of the media (newspapers, television, radio, and so on) have given the public very different messages about global climate change. Headlines have ranged from 'There's nothing to worry about, enjoy the sun!' to 'Act Now, or face Doom!'

The Intergovernmental Panel on Climate Change (IPCC) is the largest and most respected group of climate change experts, composed of the top scientists from around the world. It's message is clear: global climate change is happening now – there is no uncertainty.

A study was made of how global warming was being reported in the US. The researchers identified every serious article on global warming from the *New York Times*, the *Washington Post*, the *Los Angeles Times* and the *Wall Street Journal*. From a total of 3543 articles, the researchers examined a random sample of 636 articles. They found that the journalists had, in most cases, deliberately tried to present two sides to the argument. This usually involved a quote from one scientist who believed global warming was artificial and one from a scientist who believed that it was natural. Thus, these top, serious newspapers were giving the impression that the world's scientists were having a rip-roaring debate on the causes of global warming when they were not!

When people are confused, they usually do one of two things: ignore everything and do nothing, or panic.

For some people global climate change just is not an issue:

12 species of insect are becoming extinct every day? 'Bugs, uuurrggh!'

Drive less, walk more? 'I can go from 0 to 60 mph in 8.4 seconds in my new car!'

Floods in Bangladesh? 'That's the other side of the planet.'

Even Prime Ministers and Presidents of countries may agree that something should be done but often disagree on what this should be!

Activity

7 Here are five quotes from five leaders. Match the quote with the leader.

All across the world, in every kind of environment and region known to man, increasingly dangerous weather patterns and devastating storms are abruptly putting an end to the long-running debate over whether or not climate change is real. Not only is it real, it's here.

President Bush's attitude to climate change is disgraceful.... The debate is over, we see the threat. The time for action is now.

If I can be blunt, Kyoto would have wrecked our economy. There was no way I could sign.

Countries like ours produce only a fraction of the total greenhouse gas emissions, and cannot afford the extra costs of cutting them. Efforts to stop climate change will affect our efforts to achieve higher GDP growth rates to eradicate poverty speedily.

Climate change should be seen as the greatest challenge to face man and treated as a much bigger priority in the United Kingdom.

Prince Charles   *US President Barack Obama*   *Arnold Schwarzenegger Governor of California, USA*   *Indian Prime Minister Manmohan Singh*   *Ex-US President George W. Bush*

Compared to the UK or the USA, India is a poor country. It wants to become richer and it wants its people to have the running water, instant electricity and health service that the wealthiest European countries have. Wealthy, western countries are asking India to burn less coal but this is exactly what the western countries did to become wealthy in the first place! Meanwhile, people in the rich west are reluctant to give up their consumer lifestyles perhaps not realising their effect on other less developed countries.

Sitting higher tier

Carbon neutral?

Biofuels are supposed to be carbon neutral. The amount of CO_2 emitted when they are burnt is equal to that which they absorbed in photosynthesis, so burning them has no **net** effect on CO_2 levels.

But some scientists think that this isn't true. They argue that two serious effects have been ignored:

1 Natural vegetation has had to be cleared to make way for the biofuels – the machinery used to do this emitted huge volumes of CO_2 and the churning up of the soil would also release CO_2.
2 Countries like the US are switching from growing food crops, e.g. wheat, to biofuels. Other countries then have to grow more wheat but are much less efficient at doing this and use a lot more land.

This means more natural vegetation has to be cleared, further increasing CO_2 emissions.

These 'hidden' emissions may mean that biofuels are anything but carbon neutral!

Activity

Mudhasser is an 18 year-old boy from Kakinada, a coastal town in Bangladesh. In the past two years his house has been washed away three times by sea flooding. He had two brothers and one sister but one brother drowned in the last flood. He has been to school for only one year since he was 14. He helps his father and neighbours catch fish every day. There are no factories in Kakinada and Mudhasser blames greenhouse gases from richer countries for his life of poverty.

Peter is an 18 year-old boy from Bristol. His parents are doctors. He lives in a big house with his three sisters and the family go abroad twice a year on holiday. He will be going to University in October, having spent seven years at a local school. Peter does not like to think about disasters in faraway countries as it makes him feel depressed.

I *Flooding in Bangladesh*

8 Imagine that Mudhasser and Peter meet. Write a short filmscript in which Mudhasser and Peter talk about some of the following:

- Why are some people rich while others live in poverty?
- Do rich western people have a duty to help poor countries develop?
- Did Peter's foreign holidays cause the flooding that killed Mudhasser's brother?

It is of course impossible to blame a flood in one country on the actions of one family in another. Global climate change is extremely complex. Even the most sophisticated computer model cannot include all the factors that influence climate change. When scientists report to politicians, they explain that their models have limitations.

The UK has both domestic and international targets for reducing climate change:

Kyoto Protocol targets

At a meeting in Kyoto, Japan, many countries agreed to specific cuts in their emissions of carbon dioxide, methane, nitrous oxide and compounds containing fluorine. The UN treaty came into force in February 2005 in most of the major countries of the world.

Domestic CO_2 target

The UK is aiming, by 2010, to cut domestic emissions of carbon dioxide to 20 per cent of the level they were in 1990.

UK Climate Change Act

The UK must reduce greenhouse gas emissions by at least 80 per cent by 2050, and carbon dioxide emissions by at least 26 per cent by 2020, both set against emissions in 1990.

Sitting higher tier

Both the US and Australia refused to sign the Kyoto Protocol. President Bush believed that achieving such cuts in emissions would put thousands of US workers out of jobs when power stations, automobile manufacturers, and so on went bust. The Australian Prime Minister was worried that achieving the required cuts was impossible – Australia is the world's second biggest coal consumer! However, the situation may change under new world leaders.

It can be difficult to tackle global problems like climate change. Individuals are not sure what they should do, or how serious the problem really is. Governments have to put their own country's inhabitants first. But it is possible to get international action to solve global environmental problems – the **Montreal Protocol** is a good example of this.

Ozone (O_3) exists naturally very high up in the Earth's atmosphere. Without it, life on Earth would be very difficult. Ozone absorbs ultraviolet radiation (UV) from the Sun. If this UV reached living organisms it would cause cancer, mutation and death. In 1985 an ozone hole was discovered over the Antarctic. Scientists all over the world worked together and soon discovered that the ozone layer was being destroyed by artificial chemicals, the most important of which were CFCs (chlorofluorocarbons). CFCs were being used in aerosol cans, refrigerators and in industry.

In 1987, 27 governments signed The Montreal Protocol on Substances that Deplete the Ozone Layer. They agreed to phase out the production and emissions of CFCs and other ozone-depleting substances (ODS). The Montreal Protocol has been updated regularly and has been

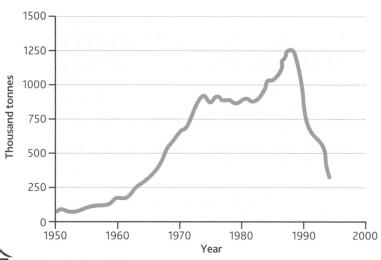

J World production of CFCs

extremely successful. Emissions of ODS have fallen (Graph **J**) and there are signs that the ozone layer is recovering!

Activity

9 Graph K shows changes in the atmospheric concentration of one type of CFC in the atmosphere and the expected changes to 2040.

    a   Name the international agreement that led to the phasing out of CFCs.

    b   Suggest why the decline in CFC concentration is slower than the initial increase.

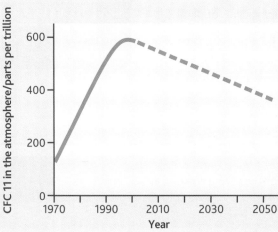

K *Levels of CFC 11*

Summary

Individuals and governments need to reduce their carbon footprints so that the worst extremes of global climate change can be avoided.

Actions to reduce the emissions and atmospheric levels of CO_2 include increased use of renewable energy, energy conservation, carbon capture and storage, carbon taxes, carbon offsetting and using carbon neutral sources of energy.

Reducing the global carbon footprint may be difficult because individuals are reluctant to change their lifestyle, or uncertain of how they should do so and governments do not want to harm their own economies.

Scientists understand that there are limitations in the ability of science to model complex processes such as climate change.

Despite these difficulties, international action can change things for the better, as the success of the Montreal Protocol has shown.

B1 The management of wildlife resources

B1.1 Why is there a need to manage wildlife?

What are the threats to wildlife?

Scientists have identified about 1.75 million different species of plant and animal on our planet. This does not include organisms such as bacteria; we do not know how many species of these there are! Worldwide, scientists discover about 15 000 new species every year (about one every 30 minutes!). Scientists believe there are between 3 and 38 million species waiting to be identified.

In this section you will learn:

about threats to wildlife

about reasons why wildlife is important.

Environmental scientists@work

New species in the Arctic

Rolf R. Gradinger is chief scientist of the National Oceanic and Atmospheric Administration's 'Hidden Ocean' expeditions. Along with other marine scientists, he has been aboard Coast Guard icebreaker Healy identifying new species that live just under the Arctic ice. So far, they have found hundreds of creatures, many never seen before, including several new species of multi-coloured jellyfish.

A *Icebreaker Healy*

When the very last individual of any species dies, the species is said to be **extinct**. Species may become extinct naturally – and millions of species undoubtedly have done over the course of evolution. Look at Diagram **B** which shows the increasing diversity of species over time. All the groups shown below the line for present day are extinct.

So if extinction is a natural process, what is the problem? It is that one particular species, humans, has accelerated the process.

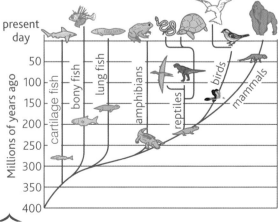

B *Living organisms over time*

Look at Graphs **C** which show the growth of the human population and the number of extinctions over time. What relationship can you see in the data?

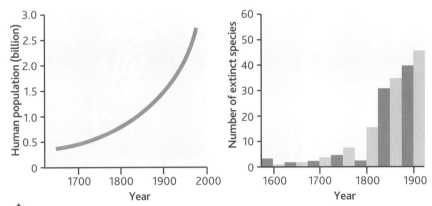

C *Growth of the human population and extinctions over time*

As the human population has increased, the number of species that have become extinct has increased. Scientists estimate that humans have increased the natural rate of species extinction by between 100 and 1000 times.

Activities

1. The human population first reached 1 billion in 1830. Now it is nearly 7 billion!

   Make a list of all the reasons why the growth of population from 1 billion to nearly 7 billion may have resulted in species being wiped out.

   You probably included some of the following in your list.
   - Pollution, e.g. oil spills can kill birds.
   - Hunting and collecting species for food, fashion, entertainment, furniture and ornaments.
   - Accidental harm from human activities such as farm harvesting, road kill and fishing **by-catch** (those fish caught by boats that are the 'wrong' species, fish that are too small, or animals such as dolphins which are just thrown back dead into the sea).
   - Disease.
   - Introduction of animals or plants that then act as **predators**, **pests**, competitors or bring disease.

2. Working in groups, prepare a short report outlining how one of the threats above is harming wildlife. Your report should explain the nature of the threat and possible solutions.

   Many scientists believe, that unless we reduce the amount of CO_2 that we are emitting, global climate change will become the biggest threat to Earth's amazing variety of plant and animal life (**biodiversity**).

Key terms

Extinct: a species for which there has been no confirmed sighting for 50 years.

By-catch: unwanted species (for example fish, turtles, dolphins) caught in fishing nets. The organisms are then thrown back, dead, into the sea.

Predator: an animal that hunts others for food.

Pest: a destructive animal which attacks crops and livestock.

Biodiversity: the number and variety of species within a region.

Tigers

Over the past 100 years, the population of tigers in the wild has decreased by 95 per cent. Fewer than 5000 now survive in the wild and several sub-species have become extinct. The biggest threat is the illegal killing of tigers to make traditional Chinese medicines. Tiger bones are used to make a broth for treating rheumatism, muscle cramps and rabies. Tiger penis soup is sold as an aphrodisiac at $320 a bowl! Tiger bristles are used to make brushes and tiger skins are used to make bags, shoes and clothing.

Status of the world's tigers

- Bali tiger   extinct, 1940s
- Caspian tiger   extinct, 1970s
- Javan tiger   extinct, 1980s
- South China tiger   20 left
- Siberian tiger   200 left
- Sumatran tiger   400 left
- Indo-Chinese tiger 1000 left
- Bengal tiger   3000 left

D *A Siberian tiger*

Polar bears in the Arctic

The biggest threat to the 25 000 polar bears that live in the Arctic used to be hunting, but now it is rising sea temperatures (Section A3.3)

Norwegian scientists working for the World Wide Fund for Nature (WWF) have attached radio collars to several bears. The collar sends a signal to a satellite. This enables the scientists to track their daily movements and to see how they respond to there being less sea ice. Already it seems that, as the number of warm days increases, the polar bears are forced to come back on to the ice earlier. This reduces the number of days they can spend hunting. In turn, this means that they have not built up sufficient fat reserves to survive the winter and the number of cubs that are being born is going down.

E *A polar bear wearing a radio collar*

AQA *Examiner's tip*

Many candidates can suggest one reason why species become extinct. However, you also need to be able to explain why the factor you have suggested results in the population being reduced to zero. Only a minority of candidates make it clear that extinction is due to the species failing to breed fast enough to replace losses due to the change they propose.

At present, the biggest, single cause of extinction is **habitat** destruction by humans to make way for housing, agriculture, mineral extraction or reservoirs. European countries have long ago destroyed most of the forests that naturally covered them to grow crops and build cities. Now LEDCs in Asia, Africa and South and Central America are doing the same.

Key terms

Habitat: the natural conditions in which an organism, animal or plant lives.

Case study

Tropical rainforest (TRF)

Rainforests are the natural vegetation over much of the tropics.

Tropical rainforests are amazingly complex and diverse ecosystems. They contain at least half of all the species of plant and animal on the planet. Some scientists believe that they may contain up to 90 per cent of all species.

The rainforests are also home to some 2 million tribal hunter-gatherers. Many of these people have a tremendous knowledge of the animals and plants living in the forest. Scientists and anthropologists (social scientists who study human society) found that some of the tribes in the Brazilian Amazon used between one-half and three-quarters of the tree species in their territory. Root extracts of some tree species are used to heal wounds, others are used to reduce fever. Investigating the chemistry of these extracts may lead to new medicines and drugs.

But these tribes are threatened by the opening up of remote areas by loggers. Already, over 90 different Amazonian tribes are believed to have died out. Tropical rainforests everywhere face serious and growing threats (see Diagram **G**).

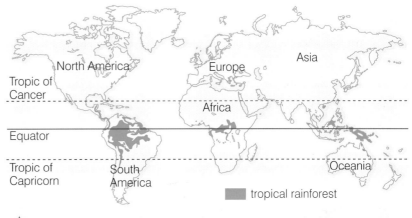

 The world's tropical rainforests

Cattle ranching
Large amounts of meat are imported into Europe from Brazil

Illegal logging
The UK is still the largest importer of illegal tropical wood in Europe!

New roads
These allow exploitation of new areas and reduce the costs of shipping and packing beef

Soybean plantations
Soybeans are used to feed cattle all over the world and are now being grown to provide biofuel

New reservoirs
These provide irrigation water for agriculture, and water for domestic and industrial use in cities

Mining
Precious metals and minerals are often present under the rainforest soils

 The rainforests face serious and growing threats

The introduction of the cane toad into Australia

The cane toad is native to South and Central America. It is an aggressive, omnivorous predator that was released into Australia to control beetles feeding on sugar cane. But it all went wrong!

The toads did not eat the beetles, but they ate lots of useful insects, such as pollinators and those that feed naturally on crop pests. In addition, the cane toad has poisonous glands over its body surface. When animals such as snakes (or dogs or most birds) try to eat the toad, they are poisoned and die.

By competing with them for food, the cane toads have also reduced the population of native frogs. The cane toad is spreading rapidly across eastern Australia and is regarded as a major threat to the environment!

H   *The cane toad*

Rhododendron

It is not just the introduction of animals that can cause environmental damage!

Rhododendron was imported from the Mediterranean by Victorian gardeners. What the gardeners did not realise was that it would outshade all of the ground plants, including tree seedlings, damage the soil and reduce the numbers of earthworms and birds.

I   *Rhododendrons in Snowdonia*

Once it is established, the rhododendron is extremely difficult to get rid of! In the Snowdonia National Park in Wales, rhododendron has threatened native juniper species. The National Park spends hundreds of thousands of pounds each year trying to clear hundreds of acres of the weed. But the plant has extremely vigorous roots and produces up to a million seeds each year. The most successful approach so far involves injecting herbicide directly into the stems of the large rhododendron bushes – this usually kills them within six months.

Losing our forests and wetlands

Mixed deciduous woodland (oak, ash, birch and hazel trees) covered about 80 per cent of the UK before humans began clearing it 4500 years ago. The woodland was chopped down and used to construct buildings, ships and tools, as well as being used for firewood.

Now, only about 1.5 per cent of these ancient woods remain and Britain is one of the least wooded countries in Europe.

These woodlands were the home or habitat of many species, for example, wild boar which, as the woodland disappeared, also became rare or extinct.

Wetlands provided another vitally important habitat, but again, humans steadily drained them in order to dry out the soil to make crop growth possible. Just as with ancient woodland, this has resulted in the decline of many species, including fen orchid, snipe and the great silver water beetle – which rely on watery habitats.

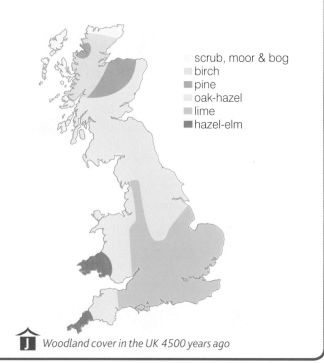

scrub, moor & bog
birch
pine
oak-hazel
lime
hazel-elm

J   *Woodland cover in the UK 4500 years ago*

Grey squirrels

Our understanding of the environment evolves. Sometimes, what seemed obvious 20 years ago, does not seem quite so obvious now!

The red squirrel is native to Britain (meaning that it has lived here for the past 350 years or so) but its population has been falling dramatically. The grey squirrel was introduced from North America in 1872 and its population has rocketed. By 2004, the population of red squirrel was 160 000 and that of the grey squirrel was 2.5 million. The connection seemed obvious to scientists. The grey squirrel, living in the same places as the red squirrel and eating the same food, was outcompeting and even attacking the red squirrel. This was the scientists' first hypothesis.

Other scientists then began to investigate populations of both red and grey squirrels in more detail.

They found that:

- wherever grey squirrels developed large populations over many years, red squirrels were usually missing
- in some areas the two species have lived together for 16 years or more
- in some areas the red squirrels had already disappeared before the grey squirrels arrived.

These last two observations made them wonder if their first hypothesis (the greys were simply out-competing the reds) was the full story! They investigated in more detail what the squirrels were eating.

They found that:

- grey squirrels digest acorns (the fruit of oak trees) more efficiently than red squirrels
- red squirrels cannot digest acorns properly and lose weight if they are fed just acorns.

This finding was a bit of a shock for many conservationists. Before this, they had been arguing that many conifer forests (for example spruce, fir and pine) should be chopped down and replaced with native oaks because it was better for wildlife. The new research suggested that this is just what grey squirrels would prefer. As a result of this, conservationists began to seriously consider felling the native oak trees in areas where the red squirrel was doing well.

The research continues…

K   *The native red squirrel*

L   *The North American grey squirrel*

Activities

Table **M** shows estimates of the population of elephants in Sri Lanka, a country in Asia.

M

Year	Estimated number of elephants in Sri Lanka
1815	30 000
1900	12 000
2003	2 800

3 Use data from the table to calculate the percentage decrease in the number of elephants between 1815 and 2003.

Diagram **N** shows some of the reasons for the decrease in the number of elephants in Sri Lanka.

4 The human population of Sri Lanka is increasing quickly. Use information from the diagram to help you explain why this may cause the decrease in the population of elephants.

Source: AQA, 2005

N

Poachers kill elephants to sell their tusks as ivory

Forests cleared to provide more farmland

Decreasing population of elephants

Angry villagers kill elephants

Area of elephants' natural habitat is reduced

Elephants cause damage to crops and houses and kill and injure villagers

Logging of forests

Elephants visit farmland and villages in search of food

■ Why is wildlife important?

Animals and plants are interdependent. Neither could exist without the other.

Plants carry out photosynthesis. This provides food for herbivores, which in turn are eaten by animals. Photosynthesis created the initial oxygen on the planet and maintains it at about 21 per cent in the atmosphere today. This allows aerobic respiration. So, in these ways, every animal on Earth is dependent on plants.

> *One quarter of western medicine's prescribed drugs, and as many as half of the 25 top-selling drugs, come from compounds discovered first in plants*
> *Plantlife International*

But plants need animals too – for the carbon dioxide that they release in respiration and for pollination and seed dispersal. So the animal and plant kingdoms are interdependent and that is perhaps the ultimate reason that humans need to ensure that we stop pushing species to extinction.

In any case, many people believe that destroying nature is morally wrong. They argue that we do not have the right to drive a species to extinction and we have an obligation to look after the planet for the next generation.

Case study

Western black rhino

On 7 July 2006, The World Conservation Union declared that this subspecies had become extinct. No one living on Earth, nor their children, will ever see a live western black rhino again. They're gone. How does this make you feel?

The now extinct western black rhino

There are powerful economic reasons too why we need to conserve species. Humans exploit the animal and plant kingdoms for a huge number of products including food, timber, resins, oils and fibres. Wild varieties of plants and animals contain valuable genes that can be used in breeding programmes designed to improve our crops and livestock. Scientists have only studied a fraction of the planet's plants, but already they have discovered many that have valuable medicinal properties that can be used to make drugs which treat diseases and cancers. For example, the rosy periwinkle (Photo **P**) grows only in Madagascar and contains powerful anticancer compounds that are used to treat testicular cancer and Hodgkin's disease.

Finally, nature is a huge source of enjoyment for people. This might be as simple as watching the birds on a garden feeder or as hair-raising as whale-watching, which, along with many other aspects of eco-tourism, generates money that can be used to help conserve species and their habitats. These are described as aesthetic reasons for conserving wildlife (an aesthete is a pleasure-seeker).

P   *Rosy periwinkle*

Activity

5   Imagine that you are the minister in charge of Forest Resources in a tropical country. Part of your job is to generate income from the large area of mountainous rainforest that is within your borders. The rainforest is teeming with wildlife and may contain previously undiscovered species. It is also home to several tribes.

The money is going to be used to help the country develop an efficient road system and pay for a national water treatment system. You need to generate income every year for the foreseeable future.

Working with a partner, draw up a list of all the ways that you could generate income from the forest. For each method, identify its advantages and disadvantages in a table like this one below. One way has been completed for you.

How the rainforest can generate income	Advantages	Disadvantages
Sell it all to a logging company	Will generate a lot of money immediately	There will be no income in future years The native tribes will lose their home Biodiversity will be destroyed Rainfall flowing off the bare mountains may flood the cities in the lowlands

Summary

Extinctions are a normal part of evolution but humans have accelerated the rate of extinction of other species.

The major threats to wildlife include habitat destruction, global climate change, hunting and collecting and the introduction of new species.

Animals and plants co-exist in a state of interdependence.

Humans need to conserve wildlife to maintain this interdependence but also because there are strong moral, economic and aesthetic reasons to do so.

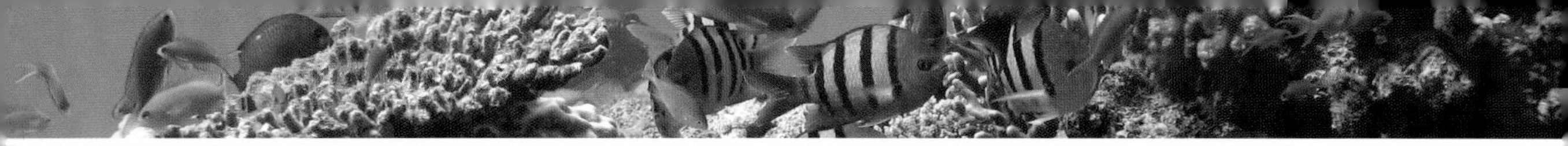

B1.2 How is wildlife conserved?

In this section you will learn:
- how to identify organisms, estimate populations and sample the environment using a transect
- about the work of conservation organizations
- about conservation agreements
- about the work of nature reserve wardens.

How do conservationists identify 'at risk' species and habitats?

In the UK, there are about 2300 species of plants and ferns. To work out which of these need protecting the most, plant scientists monitor the size of plant populations.

How science works

Sampling

Imagine that you are working as a volunteer with Plantlife. The farmer who owns the land surrounding an ancient woodland has been spraying herbicides to kill weeds and there is a danger that some of the spray has drifted into the wood, possibly harming the bluebells that grow there. Your first task is to work out how many bluebells there are in the wood. As soon as you are inside the wood, you see huge swathes of bluebells – it looks like there are hundreds of thousands of them and you've only got one morning!

Do you?

A Give up and go home.

B Start counting them one-by-one and hope.

C Count how many there are in a small, measured area, and then do some simple maths.

Hopefully, you picked **C**! You'll need to measure a small sample of the woodland using randomly placed quadrats.

Environmental scientists@work

Plantlife

Plantlife are a charity that works to protect Britain's wild plants, fungi, lichens and the habitats in which they are found. Part of their work involves monitoring the populations of 100 species that they have identified as at risk.

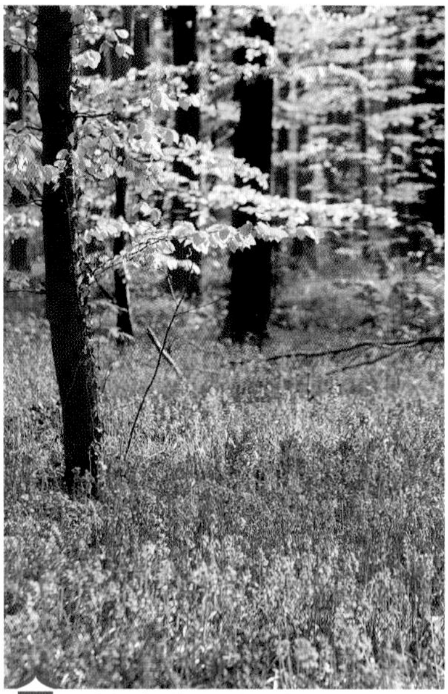

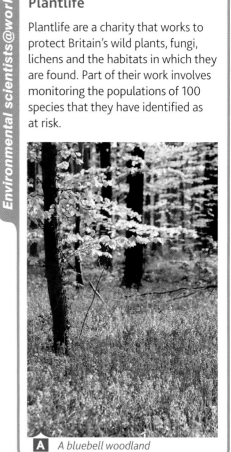

A *A bluebell woodland*

Using quadrats

A quadrat is a square metal or wooden frame of known area, usually 0.25 m², 0.5 m², or 1.0 m². They are often subdivided by crosswires into smaller squares to make it easy to count the plants.

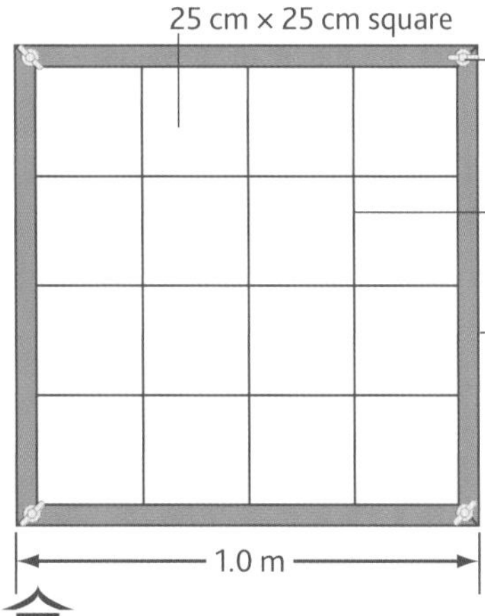
25 cm × 25 cm square
winged nut allows quadrat to be collapsed for easy carrying
wire
metal or wooden frame
1.0 m

B *A 1 m² quadrat*

Pairs of random numbers are generated on a calculator. These pairs of numbers are the coordinates where you place the quadrat in the wood. At each location, the number of bluebells is counted in each quadrat.

links

Visit the Plantlife website at **www.plantlife.org.uk**

So imagine that you used a 0.5 m² quadrat and took 10 samples in the woodland. You already know that the total area of the woodland is 4200 m².

See Table **D** for your recordings.

So, there are 140 bluebells in 10 quadrats, each of which was 0.5 m².

So that is 280 bluebells in 1 m².

So in 4200 m² there would be 4200 × 280 = 1 176 000 bluebells! Good job you didn't pick option B!

Sampling like this is a fast, easy way to get an estimate of the size of a plant population that would be impossible to count.

C   *Area of the woodland*

50 m

84 m

D	
Quadrat number	No. of bluebells
1	13
2	18
3	6
4	16
5	12
6	0
7	24
8	20
9	18
10	13
Total	140

Identifying organisms using keys

Of course, before using quadrats to estimate the population of a plant, it must be identified. Simple keys are often helpful. By looking at the organism and then working through the key until the organism is identified.

Try identifying this leaf.

1   leaf is made up of several small leaflets...................... go to 2

    leaf is made up of one large section............................ go to 3

2   leaflets are broad and flat... species A

    leaflets are narrow and hair-like.................................... species B

3   leaf has a jagged edge..species C

    leaf has a smooth edge..species D

    Did you identify it as species **D**? If so, well done!

How science works

Using transects

Sometimes, the investigation is into how plant or animal populations or soil conditions, for example, change across an area. To do this, sampling is by using a belt transect. A tape measure is laid along the sampling line. Quadrats are then placed along this line and findings in these quadrats are recorded. The transect can be continuous – where each quadrat is placed immediately in front of the last one – or interrupted, if the distance to be covered is too great for continuous quadrats.

This is a good technique to use for recording changes of plants up a beach, for example, or to investigate whether pollution from a road is affecting the plants growing in an adjacent woodland.

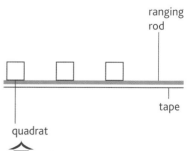

ranging rod

tape

quadrat

E   *Belt transect using interrupted quadrats*

Measuring abiotic factors

Abiotic factors are non-living factors that affect the numbers or distribution of living organisms in an area, for example, how soil pH or soil moisture content affects the number of earthworms in the soil. Soil pH and moisture content are examples of abiotic factors.

F *Examples of abiotic factors influencing populations in habitats*

Habitat	Abiotic factor that will influence living organisms in the habitat
Stream	Temperature, current velocity, depth, oxygen content
Woodland	Light levels on woodland floor, humidity of leaf litter, wind speed
Grassland	Soil pH, soil moisture content, soil nutrient content, soil clay content
Sea shore	Amount of time organism is submerged, salt content of sand or soil

Soil pH is a measure of how acidic or alkaline the soil is. This is important for two reasons. Firstly, it determines how soluble some vital plant nutrients are in the soil – plant roots can only absorb nutrients in solution. Secondly, earthworms that are crucially important in recycling nutrients, prefer slightly alkaline soil.

Soil pH can be measured either with soil test kits or electronic pH sensors.

Wind speed can be measured with an anemometer.

The moisture of a soil is important for several reasons. Firstly, plants need to be able to absorb soil moisture in order to grow. But too much water in the soil will cause problems because very wet soil holds little oxygen, which is essential to allow plant roots and invertebrates such as earthworms to respire.

G *A soil pH meter*

H *An anemometer*

Measuring the moisture content of soil:

1 Obtain a soil sample.

2 In the lab, weigh the soil sample.

3 Dry the soil sample in an oven at about 110 °C.

4 Reweigh the sample.

5 Return the sample to the oven.

6 Reweigh and repeat this process until there is no further change in mass.

7 Find the moisture content (WC) by subtracting the final mass from the original mass (OM).

8 $\dfrac{WC}{OM} \times 100$ = percentage moisture content.

Sitting higher tier

Measuring humidity

The amount of water in the air – humidity – where plants are growing also affects the growth of important indicator species such as lichens. Usually, relative humidity (the percentage present of the amount of water that could be held in the air as vapour at that temperature) is measured with an electronic sensor.

When measuring any of these abiotic factors, high quality instruments will give the accuracy needed. If more than one person is going to be taking measurements of the same factor, each instrument must have the same sensitivity. For example, when weighing soil samples on three different balances in the lab, each balance must be capable of detecting the same smallest difference, for example, 0.1 g. If one balance was only capable of measuring to the nearest gram, whilst the other two were capable of measuring to a tenth of a gram, the results would be imprecise.

I *An electronic humidity sensor*

Activity

1 Diagram **J** shows five mammals (not drawn to scale).

Use the key to identify each of these mammals.

1 tail more than half that of body length................................ go to 2
tail less than half that of body length.............................. go to 4

2 ears at top of head, with thick tail................................... *Sciurus caroliniensis* (grey squirrel)
ears at side of head, with thin tail................................... go to 3

3 nose pointed, nose length longer than its depth....................... *Sorex araneus* (common shrew)
nose blunt, nose lenth shorter than its depth............................. *Clethrionomys glareolus* (bank vole)

4 front legs as wide or wider than long................................. *Talpa europaea* (common mole)
front legs longer than wide... *Oryctolagus cuniculus* (European rabbit)

J

How can zoos, botanic gardens and seed banks help in conservation?

As the human population increases, more and more of the natural habitat of wild animals is being destroyed to make way for cities, roads and agriculture. This has pushed thousands of species towards extinction. One of the aims of zoos is to keep a sample of these animals in captivity, allow them to breed and then, hopefully, return them to the wild once the threats to their habitats have been resolved.

> Zoos exploit animals for entertainment and the conditions that the animals live in are often cramped and nothing like the animal's natural environment. Captive breeding and reintroduction programmes are rarely successful.

> Zoos provide a safe haven for threatened species. They provide a way of studying animal behaviour and captive breeding programmes can build up the populations of endangered species.

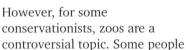 **K** *Arguments for and against zoos*

However, for some conservationists, zoos are a controversial topic. Some people believe that zoos are simply exploiting animals and distracting us from the real problem – that of habitat destruction (see Diagram **K**).

The International Union for the Conservation of Nature (IUCN) has identified groups of species that are particularly at risk – for example, those that only live in just one or two areas of the world, those of high economic value and those at the top of food chains.

The IUCN encourages zoos to capture a proportion of these species to try to establish **captive breeding** populations. The aim is to build up the numbers of the species and then reintroduce them to the wild at a later date.

There are now more than 3000 captive breeding programmes around the world. **Stud books** are used to monitor the history (diet, health, matings) of many captive individuals, allowing recommendations to be made about which individuals should be allowed or encouraged to mate. Rare animals are exchanged internationally between co-operating zoos in an effort to increase the genetic diversity of the offspring.

However, captive breeding and reintroduction faces some serious problems:

- The species must be able to survive in its original habitat and this becomes more unlikely the longer an individual is kept in captivity. Wild animals may just get used to the zoo environment and become tame.

- Some aspects of an animals' behaviour are learned and some they are born with (the behaviour is said to be **innate**). The proportion of learned behaviour increases from primitive invertebrates to fish to reptiles to mammals. Thus, primates such as the golden lion tamarin must have a chance to spend time with and learn from experienced adults when they are young. If they are not given the opportunity to learn that snakes or poisonous figs, for example, are dangerous, their release into the wild could be disastrous!

- Captive breeding often only begins when the wild population has fallen to very low numbers. This means that the genetic diversity of the captive population is usually very low. The lower the genetic diversity, the more unlikely it is that breeding will be successful.

Key terms

Captive breeding: the breeding of species in captivity, usually zoos, with the aim of reintroducing the animals back to their original habitat once it is safe to do so.

Stud book: an international register, updated every 3 years, which lists all captive individuals of a species which is under threat.

- Captive breeding is very expensive. Some scientists estimate that the cost of keeping African elephants in captivity is 50 times that of maintaining equivalent populations in National Parks in Zambia.

The problem of disappearing habitat is not being solved so we are in danger of having nowhere to reintroduce these animals.

Despite these problems, animal scientists are trying to make captive breeding and reintroduction work and there have been some great success stories!

Solving the problems of captive breeding

L

Problem	Solution
Few animals available to choose from for mating	Begin programme before population reaches low levels
High mortality due to stress	Keep populations as high as possible and maintain realistic habitats
Species lose their ability to survive in the original habitat	Recreate real habitat as far as possible
Low genetic diversity of the captive population	Breed between zoos and maintain stud books
Little opportunity for development of learned behaviours, e.g. of food supplies or predators from parents, so individuals are unable to survive when released	Maintain families/different age ranges
Expensive	Educate zoo visitors about the benefits of captive breeding and increase the entry fees

Reintroducing the red kite

The red kite (*Milvus milvus*) used to be a very common bird in Britain but it became extinct in England through human persecution. In 1989, scientists working for Natural England released 10 kites that had been imported from Sweden, at a secret location in the Chiltern Hills (Map **O**). Unfortunately, the red kites all flew home and failed to return the next year!

The scientists realised that they needed kites that would not migrate. Over the next 5 years, kite chicks from Spain were flown over and released. The kites have bred and their populations have rocketed – the release programme has been extremely successful (see Graph **N**).

M *The red kite*

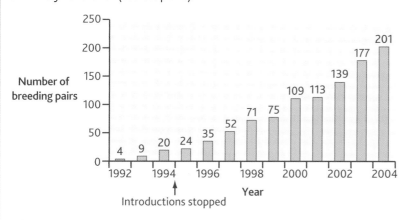

N *Breeding pairs of red kites in the Chilterns 1992–2004*
Source: The Southern England Red Kite Group

O *The Chilterrn Hills*

Environmental scientists@work

3 The golden lion tamarin is a small monkey living in coastal tropical rainforests in Brazil (Photo **P**). Over the past 100 years, much of this forest has been destroyed to make way for urban expansion. A captive breeding programme was established and the tamarin is now being reintroduced into the wild.

   a Explain why some species do not breed successfully in captivity.

   b Even if an animal successfully breeds in captivity, its reintroduction to the wild may fail. Explain why.

Botanic gardens are a vital way of helping to conserve plants. Besides growing actual living specimens, they also preserve plants as seeds and tissue cultures. Some botanic gardens concentrate on particular types of plants – food crops or medicinal plants, for example – while others aim to collect every species from a particular region or country.

The research that they conduct into ways of storing seed and growing plants is shared around the world when it is published in scientific journals.

Seed banks collect seeds from important species, for example, crops and then dry and freeze them. Such seeds can then be stored indefinitely. If, for some reason, crops are then wiped out in an area, the seeds can be allowed to warm up and germinate so that the crop can be replaced.

P *A golden lion tamarin*

Environmental scientists@work

The Millenium Seed Bank Project

Plant scientists at Kew Gardens in Surrey are collaborating with dozens of colleagues all over the world in The Millennium Seed Bank Project. Their aims are big and bold!

- Collect and protect 24 000 plant species from around the globe against extinction.
- Collect and conserve seeds from every UK plant.
- Carry out research to improve all aspects of seed conservation.
- Make seeds available for research and species reintroduction into the wild.

The UK Programme has already collected seed from over 95 per cent of the UK's native higher plants.

4 Suggest four benefits of preventing plant species from becoming extinct.

How is nature conservation organised in the UK and internationally?

Whose job is it to look after wildlife and their habitats in the UK? The answer is 'a huge range of organisations'!

Our government employs thousands of scientists across many disciplines (pollution protection, wildlife and water resource management, agriculture, forestry) who work together to protect our wildlife. All the governments of MEDCs have similar teams of experts. There are also hundreds of non-government organisations (NGOs) who also employ scientists to monitor the environment. Some of these are based just in the UK, but some are international. NGOs investigate conservation issues, collect evidence and produce scientific reports which they use to try to influence the government's decisions.

Government and non-government conservation organisations

Organisation	Government organisation (GO) or non–government organisation (NGO)	Activities
Environment Agency	GO	Protect and try to improve the environment in England and Wales. 'It's our job to make sure that air, land and water are looked after by everyone in today's society, so that tomorrow's generations inherit a cleaner, healthier world'. The Environment Agency employs 12 000 people and spends £900 million every year on activities such as flood prevention, habitat protection and pollution control.
Natural England	GO	Works for people, places and nature to conserve and enhance biodiversity, landscapes and wildlife in rural, urban, coastal and marine areas. Conserves and enhances the natural environment for its intrinsic value, the wellbeing and enjoyment of people, and the economic prosperity it brings. Increases opportunities to make the natural environment an enriching part of people's everyday lives, and improve its long term security by contributing to the sustainable management of natural resources.
RSPB	NGO	The RSPB is the UK charity working to secure a healthy environment for birds and other wildlife, helping to create a better world for us all. This is in the belief that bird populations reflect the health of the planet. They are the largest wildlife conservation organisation in Europe. They rely upon memberships and donations to fund work and this dictates the scale of their conservation success.
WWF	NGO	The planet's leading conservation organisation. Mission is to stop the degradation of the planet's natural environment and to build a future in which humans live in harmony with nature, by: • conserving the world's biological diversity • ensuring that the use of renewable natural resources is sustainable • promoting the reduction of pollution and wasteful consumption.

Activity

5   Use the internet to find the jobs sections of each of these organisations to see what sorts of jobs they have available.

Fisher's estuarine moth

Scientists working for the Environment Agency are helping to try to save the only remaining population of Fisher's estuarine moth (Photo **R**).

A national trapping programme found that a few of the remaining individuals live in low-lying areas on the north Essex Coast near Walton-on-the-Naze (Map **S**). Using sampling techniques, the scientists estimated that the total population was somewhere between 1000 and 1500.

The scientists studied the life cycle, feeding habits and predators of the moth to try to identify the threats which the species faced. They found that the three really important factors were:

R *Fisher's estuarine moth*

Walton-on-the-Naze

S *The location of a Fisher's estuarine moth population*

1 The caterpillars of the moth only feed on one type of plant – Hog's fennel (Photo **T**) – and one plant can only support one caterpillar.

2 All of the existing moth habitats are at risk of flooding if sea levels continue to rise because of global climate change.

3 The moths don't migrate around the country – in fact they hardly ever move more than 10 m away from the Hog's fennel plant that they fed on as a caterpillar!

The scientists have put together a Survival Plan for the moth. The moth was already protected under the Wildlife and Countryside Act but since October 2008, the moth and its habitat are protected under EU legislation. Local farmers have been paid to plant Hog's fennel and spread seed and have agreed to cut grass only in late autumn when there is little chance that the moth or its caterpillars will be harmed. Eggs of Fisher's estuarine moth have subsequently been introduced via a captive breeding programme and ten new areas of habitat have been created. Recent monitoring suggests that the moth is now spreading away from areas that will flood – the Survival Plan looks like it's working!

T *Hog's fennel*

This is a good example of how scientists identify species at risk. In order to do this they need to estimate regularly the species':

- Population size.
- Age distribution of individuals. What proportion are young enough to be able to breed?
- Sex ratio. There should be roughly equal numbers of males and females.

Sitting higher tier

Identifying species at risk

There are three other characteristics that scientists consider when they are deciding which animal species are at risk:

- Position in the food chain. Organisms at the top of a food chain are always rarer than those at the bottom. In the 1970s large numbers of peregrine falcons were found dead. These magnificent birds of prey are at the top of the food chain and the subsequent scientific investigation showed that a pesticide, which was subsequently banned, had poisoned them.

- Tolerance range. If conditions change slightly, how well can the species adapt? There is already strong evidence that, because of global climate change (Section A3.3), many species are having to move north to seek cooler temperatures.

- Migration habits. Migration may increase or decrease a species' chance of survival. Many species of bird that spend the summer in England fly across Africa in search of winter sun! But what if the deserts in Africa continue to expand? Will the birds have sufficient energy and food and water supplies to reach their destination?

U *Peregrine falcon*

Case study

Dormice corridors

Scientists from Natural England are working with Wildlife Trusts and farmers in several counties in England to try to create wildlife corridors to help encourage the spread of dormice. Dormice are tiny, nocturnal animals that feed on flowers, nuts, pollen, fruits and some insects (especially aphids and caterpillars) (Photo **V**).

Dormice have a very restricted distribution and have become extinct in seven counties (Map **W**).

The major cause of this has been the loss and fragmentation of deciduous woodland. However, they will also live in hedgerows, especially wide ones that have many different plant species growing in them. The aim is to recreate these types of hedgerows in order to provide a link or corridor between isolated plots of woodland. It is hoped that this will encourage the dormice to spread back into the counties from which they have been lost.

V *A dormouse*

W *Dormice distribution*

Environmental scientists from many countries have worked together to create conservation management initiatives to protect valuable habitats as well as wildlife.

Conservation initiative	Description and aims
CITES (Convention on International Trade in Endangered Species)	An international agreement between governments of 160+ countries
	Prohibits commercial trade in endangered wild animals and plants and products made from them
Ramsar Convention	An international agreement that commits most of the world's governments to conserve important wetland areas. These sites are particularly important for bird conservation

In the UK, National Parks such the Lake District have been set up to protect the landscape of the area – mountains, rivers, sheep pastures and distinctive towns. But in other countries, such as Kenya, in Africa, the main purpose of National Parks is to conserve wildlife and their habitats.

Environmental scientists@work

On safari

Kenya has 22 National Parks and 28 National Reserves. Wildlife tourism is the biggest source of income in Kenya but mass safari tourism needs careful management – tourists rampaging all over the country in 4x4s would change animal behaviour and threaten habitats. The World Conservation Society employ full-time scientists who study the impact of tourism on Kenya's wildlife. They also study ways of reducing conflicts in areas where agriculture and wild habitat overlap – if local people do not benefit from wildlife conservation, they will not see the point of cooperation.

One problem is that prized wildlife such as lion, hyena, wild dog, cheetah and leopard prey on domestic livestock that live outside of protected areas. WCS scientists are using radio and GPS satellite collars to monitor the movements of these animals to try to ensure that areas designated for agriculture do not overlap with areas where these predators are likely to roam.

Y *Tourists on safari in Kenya*

Sitting higher tier

IUCN (International Union for the Conservation of Nature)

This is a network of more than 80 countries, whose scientists, planners and politicians are working together promote biodiversity and the sustainable use of resourses.

They produce Red Lists which classify species in terms of their risk of extinction and are then used by governments and NGOs to help protect the endangered species. A variety of scientists from GOs and NGO help to compile these lists.

Case study

The Iberian lynx

The Iberian lynx lives only in two isolated pockets of western Spain and is on the IUCN's red list as critically endangered. Without urgent help, it will become extinct and would be the first big cat in Europe to do so since the disappearance of the Sabre-toothed tiger 10 000 years ago. The threats include the usual suspects: expanding agriculture, towns and cities and more traffic, but global climate change is also threatening as forest fires become more common.

The IUCN scientists have put together an action plan to save the lynx. It involves strict protection of the species, educating private landowners, designating protected areas, captive breeding and release into new areas and efforts to increase the populations of its main prey – rabbits. The scientists have established a system for annually evaluating the success of the action plan which involves monitoring:

- the existing lynx population (currently between 74 and 134 individuals)
- the success of lynx reintroductions to existing and new habitats
- efforts to increase rabbit populations by planting their preferred forage species.

Z *The Iberian lynx*

Sitting higher tier

Biosphere reserves

Biosphere reserves are areas nominated by national governments and designated by UNESCO (United Nations Educational, Scientific and Cultural Organisation) which permits sustainable development to protect the livelihood of local people as well as wildlife. England has three biosphere reserves: Braunton Burrows (north Devon coast), Moor House/ Upper Teesdale (north Pennines), and on the North Norfolk coast. They are all valuable for their landscape and biodiversity but are managed so as to allow the sustainable use of natural resources by the local communities.

AA *Braunton Burrows*

■ What do nature reserve wardens do?

Nature and countryside wardens are employed in many nature reserves and National Parks. Most of the landscapes of England are not natural and need active management to keep them looking the way they do now.

Devichoys Wood Nature Reserve, Cornwall

This reserve is managed by Cornwall Wildlife Trust. The warden's main practical activity is to continue an ancient form of woodland management – **coppicing**. This involves cutting deciduous trees such as ash and hazel down to a stump. The following year, shoots will start to grow from the stump and, in this way, a single tree can live for hundreds of years. The wardens cut a different area each year. This creates a varied age and size structure within the wood, lets in plenty of light and encourages a rich diversity of woodland flowers. Insects, especially butterflies, increase in numbers in the sunny areas created by coppicing and this provides food for woodland birds.

Most of the wood that is cut is sold but some is left in small stacks around the wood to provide a habitat for invertebrates and fungi. Species such as rhododendron, sycamore and beech, that could compete for light and nutrients with the coppice trees are chopped down as soon as they are found!

Without the wardens to organise this kind of woodland management vigorous trees and invasive species would take over, cutting out the light and causing many other species of plant to die out. The woodland would be a far less diverse environment and would support fewer animal species too.

Key terms

Coppicing: a traditional ancient form of woodland management that involves cutting trees down to a stump in order to encourage the growth of several new shoots.

AB *Devichoys Wood, Cornwall*

Environmental scientists@work

AC *Coppicing*

AD *Coppicing*

Campfield Marsh, Cumbria

Campfield Marsh Nature Reserve in Cumbria is owned and managed by the RSPB. It includes one of the largest raised bogs in the UK and the wardens who work there have to actively manage the bog to prevent it becoming damaged or degraded.

As its name suggests, raised bogs are wet! The reserve contains typical bog vegetation including bog rosemary, cranberry and great sundew. To maintain this, the wardens have filled in old drains that were helping water escape and removed birch trees which were absorbing water from and drying the soil. Twenty-three hectares of new wet grassland have also been created to help raise the level of underground water. This will mean that the bog will, once again, start to create peat – waterlogged soil that helps to trap carbon away. It is hoped that the wet grassland will also become a good breeding site for birds such as lapwings, redshanks and snipe.

AE *Campfield Marsh RSPB reserve*

The work done by wardens is extremely varied and depends, to some extent, on the habitats that they are managing. Monitoring the species of plants and animals on the reserve is an on-going task. Often, simple management techniques such as setting up bird nesting boxes will have a dramatic effect on a species population. More drastic action is sometimes needed to control pests or competitors. On the Long Mynd, an area of upland bracken and heather in Shropshire, wardens have begun to shoot the crows that are believed to be responsible for the declining population of songbirds. If left unmanaged, even this upland area would slowly turn back into woodland through succession. Wardens prevent this by regularly removing invasive species such as birch and ash trees.

Most reserves are open to the public, so wardens must also be prepared to deal with visitors. Often, this will involve informing them of what to look out for and where to go.

This might involve nature trails or interpretation boards but it may also involve managing a busy visitor centre!

AF *A typical interpretation board*

Often, reserves will use zoning to manage the reserve effectively. This might involve space-zoning, for example fencing off an area where birds are known to be nesting. Time-zoning involves closing off an area for a specified period of the year, for example, to allow an area of ground to be re-seeded with the desired plant species.

Sitting higher tier

Evaluating conservation programmes

Conservation programmes cost a lot of money so it is important to be able to evaluate which techniques work and which are less successful. This can be achieved by measuring numbers of successful reintroductions and breeding, monitoring changes in population and balancing any success against the programme cost.

One tremendously successful programme involved the re-introduction of the American bison after it reached near-extinction (Photo **AG**). Find out more about this programme at **www.americanbisonsocietyonline.org**.

AG *American bison*

Activity

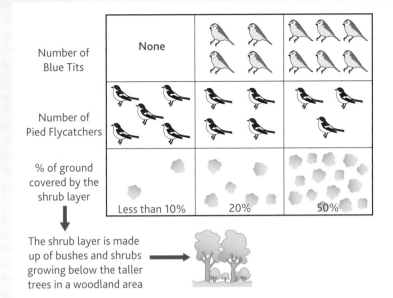

The shrub layer is made up of bushes and shrubs growing below the taller trees in a woodland area

AH

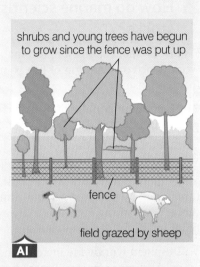

shrubs and young trees have begun to grow since the fence was put up

fence

field grazed by sheep

AI

6 The shrub layer in woodland is made up of bushes and shrubs growing below the taller trees. Blue tits and pied flycatchers are two species of birds which live in woodlands. Diagram **AH** shows how changing the percentage cover of the shrub layer can affect the numbers of these birds.

a State what happens to the number of pied flycatchers as the percentage of the ground covered by the shrub layer increases.

b State what happens to the number of blue tits as the percentage of the ground covered by the shrub layer increases.

c Many woods in Wales have only a small percentage of the ground covered by bushes and shrubs. This is because sheep graze under the trees. The sheep eat young shrubs before they can grow. They can also eat young tree seedlings. Diagram **AI** shows a field and an area of woodland in a nature reserve where pied flycatchers are a protected species. A fence has been put up to stop sheep from getting into the woodland.

Explain one possible advantage and one possible disadvantage for nature conservation if the fence is kept in place permanently.

Source: AQA, 2006

Summary

Conservationists have to prioritise which species they try to protect.

The use of keys help us to identify plants and animals and quadrats to sample them.

Transects are a good way of investigating how abiotic or biotic factors change across an area.

Environmental scientists may work for government agencies such as Natural England, non-government agencies such as the RSPB or international agencies such as the IUCN.

Zoos may carry out captive breeding of endangered populations in the hope that individuals can be reintroduced to their natural habitat.

Botanic gardens and seed banks are a vital way of helping to conserve plants.

Agreements such as CITES and the Ramsar Convention enable countries all over the world to work together to conserve habitats and biodiversity.

Nature Reserve wardens use scientific knowledge and practical skills to manage reserves.

How do marine scientists identify threatened fish stocks?

Fish is the main source of protein for millions of people and the worldwide consumption of fish is increasing. This is likely to continue for two reasons:

1 The human population is expected to continue to increase.

2 World consumption of livestock products is expected to increase rapidly and one third of all the fish caught is used to make feed for animals such as pigs, chickens and farmed fish.

Many marine scientists believe that the productivity of the oceans is threatened by pollution, global climate change and overfishing. Of these, **overfishing** is believed to have the most serious impact. They point to the following evidence:

- Despite a worldwide increase in the number of fishermen and boats in previous years, total catch has not increased.

- In many fisheries, despite the same number of boats fishing for the same number of days, total catch is decreasing rapidly.

- In many fisheries, the average size and age of fish caught has decreased – in other words, fish are being caught before they have had time to mature and breed.

> **In this section you will learn:**
>
> about the work of marine scientists
>
> about the threats to fish stocks
>
> how fishing can be made sustainable.

> **Key terms**
>
> **Overfishing**: more fish are caught than are replaced by reproduction. It is biologically and economically unsustainable.

Environmental scientists@work

Monitoring fish populations

Marine scientists working for Defra (Department for Environment, Food and Rural Affairs) use the research vessel, *Endeavour* and charter fishing boats to monitor the size and age structure of populations of key fish species around the UK coast.

Similar data is collected from samples of fish that have been landed by commercial vessels.

A *Marine scientists collect data about fish populations*

Overfishing not only threatens individual fish species, for example, cod, but also the food chains and webs of which the fish is a part. The jobs of the fishermen, processing workers and fish wholesalers – the fishery as a whole, are also endangered.

North Sea cod

Cod do not start to breed until they are 4 years old but they can live to the grand old age of 40! A healthy population of cod would contain many individuals of all ages and this is one of the key pieces of data that interests fishery scientists. Recently, scientists have found that only 10 per cent of the individuals in the North Sea are more than 1 or 2 years old and less than 0.5 per cent are 5 years old or more. In simple terms, this means that, out of every 200 cod, they are only finding about one individual that is old enough to breed! Overfishing has reduced the number of older, larger, mature cod.

B   *A cod*

Scientists have been urging governments to stop all cod fishing in the North Sea until stocks can recover. But every year, governments have refused. Why? Because that would mean that even more fishermen would lose their jobs.

The state of world fish stocks are assessed by scientists working at the Food and Agriculture Organisation (FAO) that is based in Rome.

In 2005, FAO's marine scientists estimated that:

- 3% of all fish stocks were underexploited
- 20% were moderately exploited
- 52% were fully exploited with no room for further expansion
- 17% were overexploited
- 7% were depleted
- 1% were recovering from depletion.

Since the FAO started monitoring the global state of stocks in 1974, there has been a steady increase in the proportion of stocks that are being overexploited or that are depleted. In the past few years, however, there are signs that this trend has stabilised and this may provide evidence that we are, at last, beginning to manage some fisheries in a more sustainable way.

Activity

1   Scientists working for the International Council for the Exploration of the Sea (ICES) assessed the current state of the major EU fisheries. Some of their results are shown in the table.

Area	No. of stocks	No. of stocks assessed	No. of stocks fished sustainably	No. of stocks overfished
North Sea, Eastern Channel, Skagerrak and Kategat	23	12	4	8
West of Scotland	10	3	1	2
Western waters	26	14	1	13
Iberian Atlantic	11	7	2	5
Baltic sea	13	2	0	2
Total	83	38	8	30

a   Calculate the percentage of stocks that were assessed.

b   Calculate the percentage of assessed stocks that have been overfished.

c   Suggest what data the scientists would have collected to identify those fisheries that have been fished unsustainably.

Why are fish stocks endangered?

Over the past 50 years, humans have become extremely efficient at catching fish.

In 2004, the world fishing fleet landed 94 million tonnes of fish. China, Peru and the United States of America were the top producing countries.

The increasing catch between 1950 and 1990 was due to several factors:

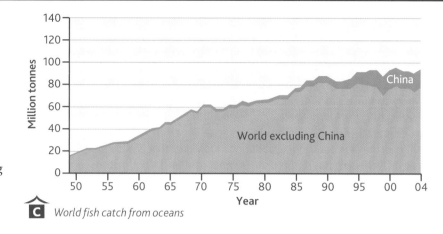

C *World fish catch from oceans*

- An increase in the number, size and power of fishing vessels.
- Increased use of lighter and stronger nets, which could therefore be made much larger.
- The development of sophisticated sonar that enabled boats to locate shoals.
- The development of huge refrigerated factory ships that could spend weeks at sea without the fish going off.

Changes in fishing

The use of drift nets and bottom trawls by fishing fleets has been particularly harmful.

Drift nets can be enormous – kilometres long – and catch and kill everything in their path. So, even if a vessel is only allowed to catch one species, it may end up killing thousands of non-target species (called by-catch) which are thrown back into the sea. Similarly, trawl nets that are dragged along the ocean floor catch everything, uproot plants and damage the sea-bed, destroying the habitat of many species in the process.

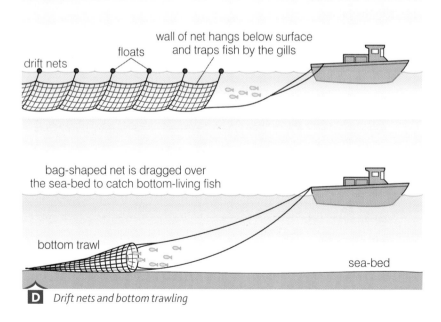

D *Drift nets and bottom trawling*

Something to consider

One quarter of all the fish eaten by humans in 2007 were not caught at sea – they were farmed in huge tanks. Unfortunately, these fish are fed using wild fish such as anchovy, herring and mackerel caught at sea. On average, it takes 2.5 kg of wild fish (or meal as it is known) to grow 1 kg of farmed fish. Fish farming used to be hailed as a way of reducing pressure on wild fish stocks. Now it is just the opposite!

One of the reasons that overfishing is a difficult problem to solve is because vessels from several countries often operate in the same fishery. So, in the North Sea, it is not unusual to have ships from Scotland, Norway, Denmark and Spain all trying to catch, for example, haddock. Each vessel has its **Total Allowable Catch** (TAC) of haddock and any other species under the EU Common Fisheries Policy. But the captains of the ships do not trust each other. If the captain of the Scottish ship obeys the law and does not go over his limit, how can he be sure that the Danish captain will do the same? Although many checks are made at the port, it is impossible for fishery officers to check every landing. Many scientists think that fishing vessels land a lot more fish than they say they do!

E   *A fish trawler*

Marine pollution

The main sources of marine pollution are:

- Organic nutrients from sewage and agriculture are decomposed by bacteria that use up much of the oxygen in the water, killing most other organisms.

- Inorganic nutrients such as nitrates and phosphates, applied as fertilisers, cause blooms of microscopic floating plants (algae) which shade life below, reducing photosynthesis. As a result, biodiversity decreases and oxygen is used up by the bacteria decomposing the dead matter.

- Sediments from mining and dredging make the water cloudy, preventing photosynthesis and clogging the gills of fish.

- Oil from tankers and other shipping. Even low levels can kill fish larvae and cause disease in marine wildlife. Oil slicks poison and suffocate wildlife. Birds are unable to fly and eventually drown.

- Plastics from old fishing nets, cargo, beach litter and industry. Many organisms become trapped in discarded nets and drown.

F   *An oil slick*

Fishing effort is the size of a fishing fleet and the number of days the fleet spends fishing. Marine scientists investigated the age-distribution of fish in two fisheries, one of which had been fished with a high effort and one which had been fished with low effort. Table **G** shows their results.

The data from the high fishing effort area has been converted into a bar chart (Graph **H**).

2 Draw a bar chart to show the data from the low fishing effort area.

The fishing fleets operating in the North Sea are controlled by EU laws. However, fisheries in the open sea are owned by no one and it is very difficult to monitor how these are being exploited. Even carefully regulated fisheries can be exploited by pirate fishing vessels.

Overfishing does not just result in declining yields. The removal of most of the population of one species will affect many others – those that it had competed with for food and the species that it fed on, for example, but little research has been done so far on these effects.

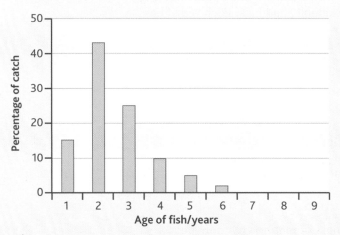

G

	Age of fish/years								
	1	2	3	4	5	6	7	8	9
Percentage of catch in high fishing effort area	15	43	25	10	5	2	0	0	0
Percentage of catch in low fishing effort area	2	3	4	4	8	10	18	40	11

H *High fishing effort*

Global climate change and fish stocks

Marine scientists are increasingly concerned about the possible effects that global climate change might have on fish stocks. It is clear that, in some areas of the world, oceans are getting warmer. Scientists have investigated whether temperature changes in the North Sea and Irish Sea have influenced cod stocks.

Cod prefer cold water. Scientists have already observed that the warming of the North Sea appears to have resulted in the cod stock moving North in search of cooler water. It may also have contributed to changes in the type, distribution and mass of microscopic plants (plankton), thus affecting the food supplies of the cod. Whatever the precise reason, it is clear that cod recruitment (birth of larvae and their development into young fish) has fallen when sea temperatures are warmer than normal.

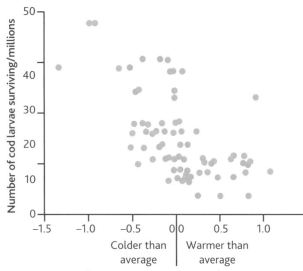

I *The effect of sea temperature on survival rates of cod larvae*

Source: Planque et al., 1998. Marine Ecology Progress Series

Cod stocks

Scientists working for the International Council for the Exploration of the Sea (ICES) monitor the size of the cod stocks in the North Sea. Each year, fishing vessels record the number of cod caught in one hour in their nets. The charts below show the results for 1984 and 2001 (Diagram **J**). The size of each circle is proportional to the number of fish caught at each site.

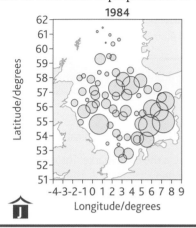
1984

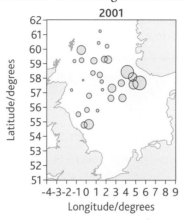
2001

J

Longitude/degrees

Source: AQA, 2005

> **Activity**
>
> **3** **a** Describe the changes to the cod stocks between 1984 and 2001.
>
> **b** In order to be able to make a valid comparison between the 1984 and 2001 data, the boats used the same fishing method and fished for the same amount of time. Suggest two other factors that would have to be kept the same for the data to be valid.

■ How can ocean fishing be made sustainable?

Scientists have collected data on fish stocks and put together action plans designed to help depleted species recover. Politicians have used these action plans to justify laws and regulations that have sometimes not gone down well with fishermen and their communities!

> **Key terms**
>
> **Quota**: the maximum weight of fish of a particular species that can be caught in a year.

Table **K** summarises the key measures that have been used to try to make fishing more sustainable.

K *Making fishing more sustainable*

Measure	How it works
Reintroduction of fish from breeding programmes	Rapidly increases the population of a particular species
Expand fish farming	Thousands of fish such as salmon can be grown in fish farms, reducing the number that need to be caught at sea
Close fisheries for a period	By banning any fishing in an area, the depleted species are given time to grow, age and reproduce
Limit the number of days that any vessel can fish	Reduces fishing effort, giving the stock time to recover
Enforce **quotas**	A **quota** is the maximum weight of fish of a particular species that can be caught in a year. After that weight has been caught, the vessels must not fish for that species again
Make the mesh size of nets bigger	This allows the small, immature fish to escape so that they can grow, age and breed
Restrict the minimum size of fish that can be landed	Only larger mature fish that have been able to breed can be landed
Restrict the size of nets, e.g. trawl nets that can be used	These nets are very destructive and catch a lot of 'waste' species (by-catch)
Provide money (subsidies) to persuade fishermen to use line-fishing techniques	Line fishing catches just the desired species and does not damage the sea-bed
Zoning	Dividing up a fishery into areas. Vessels are then only allowed to fish in a particular area, allowing the other areas to recover. Zoning can also be used to protect known breeding grounds

Continued over the page

Fleet reduction	EU fishing fleets are huge simply because, in the past, governments offered subsidies to help fishermen buy vessels and new technology, e.g. sonar
	Governments are reversing this by forcing some vessels to be scrapped
Ecolabelling	By telling consumers that a fish has been caught in a sustainably managed fishery, it is hoped that they will be persuaded to support that fishery by buying the (usually more expensive) product. By suggesting that an alternative non-threatened fish may be a suitable substitute for an endangered species
International agreements, e.g. EU Common Fisheries Policy	Each country fishing in an area is allocated a Total Allowable Catch for each species

Read the following account about a Fishery Officer whose job is to ensure fishing is kept sustainable.

Environmental scientists@work

Working for a fishery office

Sam Greene works for Lerwick Fishery Office on the Shetland Isles, Scotland. Here is his account of a typical working day.

'I leave the house at 6:30am, it is still dark outside and the wind is blowing hard. First is the daily market inspection. After a quick tally of the landings, we help to check the weights and grades of fish landed.

We then receive information from HQ that a Spanish-operated, British registered long-liner is sheltering in port. We board the long-liner and discover that this highly-equipped vessel is processing, packing and freezing its catch at sea, making inspection of the hold challenging but not impossible.

Next, we head for the Yell ferry. I observe two of the larger members of the local trawler fleet making ready to land into refrigerated containers. Following appraisal of vessels' logsheets, we carry out a full monitor of the catch, positioned in the rear of the container lorry, identifying the different species of fish as they are landed. On completion we confirm that the vessels' Skippers have accurately logged their catches.

Then it's off to a huge Hull-registered freezer trawler. The vessel has requested to be issued with an International Waters fishing licence. We have instructions to board Lerwick Port Authority's pilot boat, intercept the trawler in the channel south of the harbour and issue the licence.

Adapted from an article by the Scottish Fisheries Protection Agency www.sfpa.gov.uk © Crown copyright

Sitting higher tier

Convention for the Conservation of Antarctic Marine Living Resources

The Southern Ocean surrounds the continent of Antarctica.

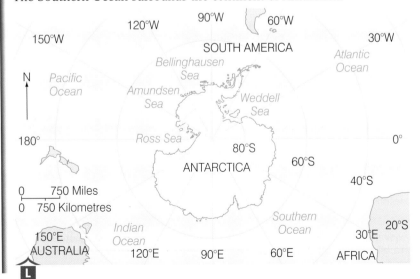

L

The Convention was established to conserve the marine life of the Southern Ocean. Scientists were concerned that if fishing vessels continued to increase their catch of krill, this could have serious effects on entire food chains, not only affecting the fish, which depend on krill for food, but also squid, birds and seals. The Convention sets out to protect the entire ecosystem rather than just individual species.

Activity

Diagram M shows a simplified food web for the Southern Ocean around Antarctica.

In the early 1990s scientists became very worried that the populations of all the whale species was in decline. In 1996, all commercial whaling was banned but whale populations did not recover.

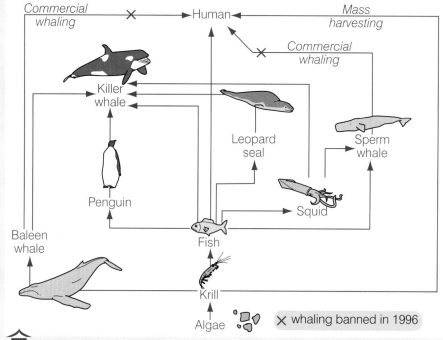

M *Food web for the Southern Ocean*

4 Use information in the food web to explain why just stopping whaling would not be enough to help whale populations recover.

Source: AQA, 2000

Summary

The oceans are under threat from pollution, global climate change and overfishing.

Scientists monitor the population sizes and age distributions of key species.

Overfishing has resulted from bigger fishing fleets, bigger and more sophisticated vessels and sonar which can detect shoals.

Overfishing is unsustainable and will lead to the collapse of fisheries unless it is stopped.

Scientists have suggested many ways to make fishing more sustainable but politicians have been slow to act upon them because this will mean job losses in the fishing industry.

B2 The management of water resources

B2.1 How is water allocated to different uses in the UK?

What is water needed for?

Water is used in almost every aspect of modern life (see Diagram **A**). Power stations use fossil fuels or uranium to heat water to produce steam. This turns turbines connected to generators that produce electricity. Industry uses vast quantities of water every day in manufacturing. Farmers irrigate crops, we use water in our homes for washing and cooking, and water resources are also important for transport, nature conservation and recreation.

Some of these uses involve removing water (**abstraction**) from a source and moving it to where it will be used. Non-abstractive uses are those where the water is not removed from its source. The four major non-abstractive uses are:

- recreation, such as sailing on reservoirs
- wildlife conservation, such as wildfowl on wetland areas
- energy, such as hydroelectricity plants
- transport, such as river barges.

What are the conflicts between different water users?

A water resource may be used for more than one thing purpose at the same time. This may result in a conflict of interest!

In this section you will learn:

what we use water for in the UK
about the conflicts between different water users
how we measure our water resources
how we monitor the effects of human activity on water resources.

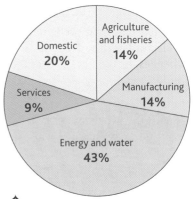

A *Use of water in the UK by sector*

B	
Use	**Potential conflicts**
Speed boats on lakes	Noise disturbs tourists and wildlife
	Danger to swimmers and wildlife
	Danger and disturbance to fishing
Sailing on reservoirs	Water pollution and conflict with anglers
Wildlife conservation on banks of reservoir	Abstraction of water causes water levels to change affecting habitats
	Boating, sailing, water-skiing may disrupt habitats
Fishing on rivers	Over-abstraction may affect breeding or movement of fish
Agriculture adjacent to rivers and around reservoirs	Runoff pollutes water

Activity

1   For each of the conflicts in Table **B**, suggest how they may be solved. Compare your suggestions with other students.

You might have suggested allocating different times to different users or space-zoning – where different activities are allowed in different parts of the lake, for example. You might even have suggested banning some activities!

Key terms

Abstraction: removing water from a source so that it can be used elsewhere.

Hydrologist: a water scientist.

Aquifer: a porous, permeable underground rock such as chalk or sandstone that contains water in millions of pores.

How are water resources measured?

Water scientists (**hydrologists**) work with geologists and use maps, GIS/remote sensing and aerial surveillance to identify all the possible sources of water in a region. To estimate how much water is actually available, they collect information on:

- rainfall
- river flow
- reservoir levels
- the volume of water that is stored underground in saturated rocks (**aquifers** (see page 125)).

The problem is that all of these volumes keep changing and global climate change is expected to significantly alter the pattern of rainfall over the UK. Over the past 40 years, winter rainfall has become more intense. There have been more frequent spells of very wet weather and an increase in total precipitation. More winter rainfall could increase the risk of flooding whereas less summer rainfall could lead to water shortages, unless there is adequate storage.

Activity

Look at the two maps in Diagram **C** which show average total precipitation (rain and snow) in summer and winter over the period 1961–1990.

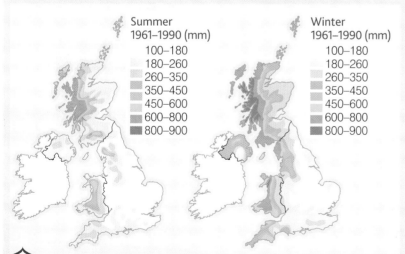

Summer 1961–1990 (mm)	Winter 1961–1990 (mm)
100–180	100–180
180–260	180–260
260–350	260–350
350–450	350–450
450–600	450–600
600–800	600–800
800–900	800–900

C   *Average total precipitation in the UK in summer and in winter, 1961–1990*

2   The highest population density and greatest demand for water is in the south-east of England in summer. What problems does this present water engineers?

Long-term measurements of precipitation, evaporation and the movement of water between sources are needed so that we can be reasonably certain that the amount of water required in a region and the country as a whole can be met by the sources of supply.

How much water?

Hydrologists working for South-East Water have produced their Water Management Plan for 2009–2025. The government is planning for up to 20 000 new homes to be built in the region. To provide energy for these, it is possible that a new coal or gas-fired power station will be needed. The power station will burn the fossil fuel to boil water to produce steam that turns the turbines that will generate the electricity for the new homes.

But how much extra water will be needed, and where is it going to come from?

Huge volumes of water will be needed by each new home. But lots of water will also be needed by the power station. Engineers estimate that it takes an average of 95 litres of water to produce 1000 kilowatt-hour of electricity. But, gas is a much more efficient fuel than coal. US scientists estimate that the most efficient gas plants need only 40 litres of water per 1000 kilowatt-hour of electricity while a coal plant might need 600 litres to produce the same amount of electricity. This is a huge range but the water scientists need to be certain that they can meet demand. Working with government plans for housing, recreation and nature conservation, hydrologists must plan decades ahead and in the south-east they are actively considering where to build very large new reservoirs.

D *Volume of water required to generate 1000 kWh of electricty*

Fuel	Volume of water (l)/ 1000 kWh electricity
Natural gas	38
Coal gasification	144–340
Coal	530–2100
Liquid natural gas	1875

Source: www.spectrum.ieee.org/apr08/6182

■ How are the effects of human activity on water resources monitored?

The Environment Agency is the UK government organisation responsible for managing water resources. The responsibilities of the scientists who work there include:

- taking care of the aquatic environment
- ensuring that all the different users of water have sufficient supplies
- trying to prevent floods
- trying to control pollution.

E *The Environment Agency works to predict and prevent flooding*

Environmental scientists@work

Predicting floods

Around 5 million people in 2 million properties live in flood-risk areas in England and Wales. Scientists working for the Environment Agency monitor the peak volumes of seven key rivers to try to predict when they are in danger of flooding. The data shown are the number of peaks in a year over a threshold specified for each river. The threshold is the level which is exceded on average three times a year during 1980 to 2000. Six of the seven rivers show an increase in the frequency of peak flows.

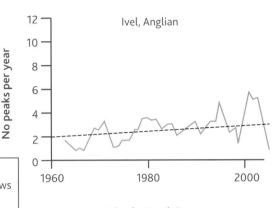

Key
— frequency of peak flows
--- frequency trend line

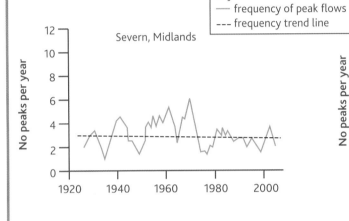

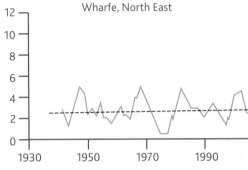

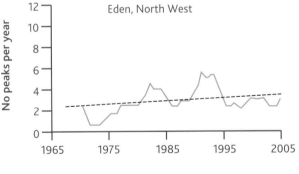

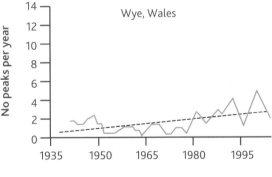

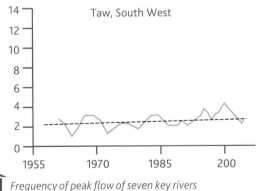

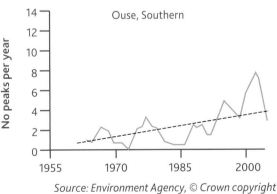

F *Frequency of peak flow of seven key rivers*

Source: Environment Agency, © Crown copyright

The Environment Agency scientists also monitor water quality. The main sources of water pollution are agriculture, industry and sewage.

Activity

3 Describe the trends shown by the graphs.

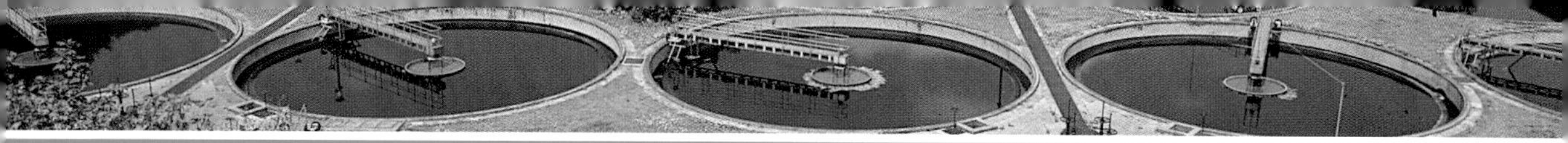

Testing water quality

Scientists from the Department for Environment, Food and Rural Affairs (Defra) consult with farmers and landowners to try to prevent fertilisers and slurry from cows polluting surface waters and aquifers.

G *Testing water quality*

Source of pollution	Description
Agriculture	Nitrate and phosphate fertilisers can cause **eutrophication** Slurry and manure can cause water to become de-oxygenated Pesticides can kill aquatic organisms directly
Industry	Toxins such as heavy metals (e.g. mercury) can be highly toxic Hot water released into rivers reduces the amount of oxygen in the water and organisms suffocate
Sewage	Heavy metals in sewage may be toxic and the organic matter may cause the water to become de-oxygenated

Key terms

Eutrophication: the artificial enrichment of water with too many nutrients such as nitrates and phosphates.

Indicator species: a common and easily identified species, e.g. an invertebrate whose presence or absence implies certain pollution levels.

AQA Examiner's tip

Don't go into the exam without knowing how to spell and define the term eutrophication!

The scientists help farmers keep up with new legislation from the EU. This puts an upper limit on the amount of nitrogen fertiliser that can be sprayed on to grassland and how much and where cow slurry can be stored. If too much nitrate gets into our drinking water, it can harm pregnant women.

Water samples from rivers, reservoirs and underground supplies are tested for nitrates, phosphates and ammonia. The presence of these substances in high concentrations may indicate that fertilisers or organic matter pollutes the water.

The scientists also monitor the types of insects and fish that live in rivers. These are extremely useful **indicators** of pollution. If organic matter pollutes a stream or river, aquatic invertebrates begin to disappear. The ones that are most sensitive to the pollution disappear first. The order in which the aquatic invertebrates disappear is shown below.

So the stonefly nymphs are very sensitive and are the first to disappear whilst the tubifex worms can tolerate quite severe pollution. By monitoring the presence, absence or changing populations of these species, the scientists obtain good evidence about the quality of the water.

up to 7–12mm
1 stonefly nymph
up to 16mm
2 flattened mayfly nymph
up to 26mm
3 caseless caddis fly larva
up to 11mm
4 swimming mayfly nymph e.g. *Baetis rhodani*
up to 20mm
5 freshwater shrimp
up to 12mm
6 waterhog louse
(7–10mm long)
7 blood worm (or midge larva)
up to 55mm
8 rat-tailed maggot
(up to 40mm long)
9 *Tubifex* worm

H *The order in which aquatic invertebrates disappear due to pollution (not drawn to scale)*

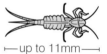

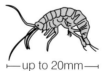

Activity

Diagram I shows scientists from the Environment Agency sampling invertebrates in a stream.

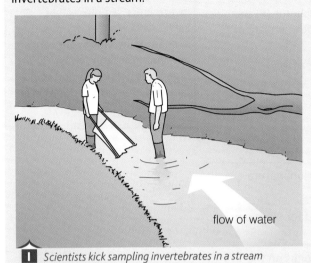

I *Scientists kick sampling invertebrates in a stream*

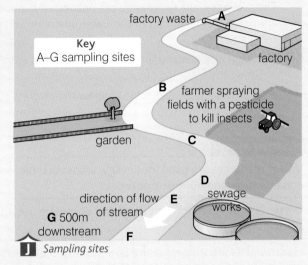

J *Sampling sites*

They used a technique called kick sampling:

- A 1m² area of the bed of the stream was marked out.
- A 1m² wide net was held by one scientist on the downstream side of the marked-out area.
- The other scientist gently scraped their boots upstream to disturb the stones on the stream bed.
- They did this for three minutes. This dislodged invertebrates that were then washed downstream into the net.
- The invertebrates were then identified, counted, and replaced downstream of the sampling site.
- They repeated this at seven sites in total.

Here are their results.

K

Invertebrate	No. of invertebrates collected at sampling site						
	A	B	C	D	E	F	G
Stonefly nymph	6	5	6	2	0	0	4
Mayfly nymph	4	4	4	3	1	0	3
Caddis fly larvae	8	6	3	4	1	1	2
Rat-tailed maggot	0	0	0	0	4	2	1
Tubifex	0	0	0	2	4	3	2

4 a Suggest a control variable in this investigation.

b Suggest why the scientists move upstream (against the current) as they take their six samples.

c The scientists were concerned that the stream was polluted by organic matter at one site. Which site do you think they suspected? Explain your answer.

Activity

5 Scientists from the Environment Agency were investigating whether a meat-processing plant was polluting the stream that ran next to it. They used test kits to measure the nitrogen (N), phosphorus (P) and ammonia (NH3) content of the water upstream and downstream of the plant.

  a Suggest how many sites should be sampled upstream and downstream of the plant.

  b Construct a suitable table to show their results.

Summary

Water resources are used for energy, transport, recreation, nature conservation and domestic purposes.

Water is abstracted for industrial and domestic use and for irrigation of crops.

Hydrologists identify, measure and monitor water supplies on the land surface (rivers and reservoirs) and those underground (aquifers).

The major sources of water pollution are agriculture, industry and sewage.

Scientists employed by the Environment Agency monitor the aquatic environment, ensure that water supply matches demand and work on flood control and pollution prevention.

B2.2 Where do supplies of drinking water come from and how are they treated to make them safe?

Where does our water come from?

The water used in households, industry, irrigation and for energy generation comes from three main sources: **aquifers**, rivers and **reservoirs**.

Geologists use sophisticated equipment to identify the aquifers that now supply about one third of the water. Aquifers are rocks such as chalk and sandstone. Aquifers have high **porosity**, i.e. a high proportion of the volume of the rock is made up of pore space that can hold water (see Diagram **A**).

Aquifer rocks must also be **permeable,** i.e. water must be able to move through it via the connected pores.

Care must be taken not to extract too much water from an aquifer as the water table, the highest level that the water reaches in the rock, will be lowered. This might cause streams that are supplied by underground water to dry up, which would kill most or all of the aquatic wildlife and damage the local scenery.

Rivers and reservoirs provide the other two thirds of water supplies. Rivers can be dammed near their source or water from rivers may be pumped into reservoirs – artificial lakes. Many reservoirs have been created by building a dam across a narrow valley in upland areas with high rainfall and impermeable rocks. Sometimes it is necessary to flood farmland and even entire villages to create reservoirs (see the Case Study on the next page).

Although the original habitat is completely destroyed, reservoirs often become valuable habitats themselves and many people regard them as attractive landscape features. Given the densely populated nature of our country, planners usually try to design reservoirs as multipurpose schemes combining water supply, nature conservation and recreation.

In this section you will learn:

where we get our water from

how planners try to match supply with demand

about water conservation

how water companies treat water to make it safe to drink.

Key terms

Aquifer: a porous, permeable underground rock such as chalk or sandstone that contains water in millions of pores.

Reservoir: an artificial lake for collecting and storing water.

Porosity: the amount of pore space in a rock.

Permeability: the rate at which water can move through the pores in a rock.

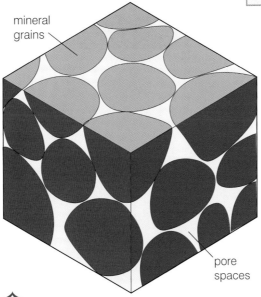

mineral grains

pore spaces

A *Aquifer rock*

Tryweryn and Capel Celyn

Despite protests, the village of Capel Celyn in the Tryweryn valley in Wales was demolished and flooded to provide drinking water for Liverpool in 1965.

Science in Society

Politicians represent the people that voted for them. They should do things that reflect their wishes. So why then, did politicians decide to completely destroy an entire village, against the wishes of the people that lived there? Sometimes, the needs of local people and the needs of society in general, conflict. Liverpool was rapidly expanding; its population was increasing and the government wanted to ensure that Liverpool remained an attractive place to live and work. The hundreds of thousands of people who worked there were a source of national wealth.

Hydrologists advised the government that the Tryweryn valley was perfect for a reservoir – long and narrow, with high rainfall and impermeable rocks. Rivers connected the valley to Liverpool, enabling easy transport of the stored water. In this case then, the politicians listened to the water scientists and decided that the national need for reliable water supplies was more important than the wishes of the villagers.

B *School children protest against the 'drowning' of their village*

C *After the Tryweryn valley was flooded to create a reservoir*

Working as a Ranger at Kielder Water and Forest Park, Northumberland

Kielder water is the largest man-made lake in the UK and is surrounded by the largest man-made woodland in the whole of Europe! It took six years to build and two years to fill with water. Besides providing the whole of the north-east with plentiful water, it attracts a quarter of a million tourists each year, offering a wide range of water-sports and hundreds of miles of cycling and walking routes.

D *Kielder Water*

As a Ranger, I assist visitors, lead events for school-parties and help maintain the paths, roads, stiles and fences in the park.

If you have spent much time walking up steep, narrow tracks in woodlands, you will know that it isn't much fun to suddenly have a mountain bike hurtling towards you at 20 mph! To solve this, we mark some tracks 'No cycles'. Similarly, some parts of the reservoir are open for water skiing, but others are not. By **space-zoning** the reservoir in this way, I help to ensure that activities such as waterskiing and line-fishing can take place at the same time.

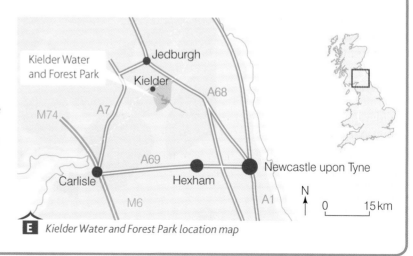

E *Kielder Water and Forest Park location map*

Activity

1 Imagine that you are a water engineer. A new town is being planned and it is your job to decide whether the water supply for the town is going to be sourced by building a new reservoir or by abstraction from the aquifer beneath it. Use the internet or textbooks for research and write a short report in the form of a table outlining the advantages and disadvantages of each method.

Hint: include information about the following:
Which will be cheapest?
Which will have greatest impact on the landscape, geology and wildlife?
Which type of water needs most treatment to make it safe to drink?

How do planners match supply with demand?

Planners need to know how much water is available in each part of the country and how much is needed, both now, and in the future.

To estimate how much water is actually available, environmental scientists collect information on rainfall, river flow, reservoir levels and the amount of water that is stored underground in aquifers. Not all of the water that falls as rain or snow will be available to use – some will be lost by evaporation or **transpiration**. Global climate change makes life difficult for hydrologists! They have to predict which areas are likely to receive more and less rainfall and assess how climate change will affect processes such as evaporation.

To assess how much water is available in aquifers, geologists measure the porosity and permeability of the rocks. This is not easy when the aquifer may be 2 km deep!

On the other side of the equation, planners need to try to predict how much water is needed. Demand for water is greatest in the heavily populated south-east of England and is expected to increase as the number of households increases. These can be planned for. But other users, such as agriculture and industry, are more difficult to predict.

Any individual or organisation that wants to abstract water has to obtain a licence from the Environment Agency.

How can we conserve water?

A lot of time, effort and money is spent abstracting and treating water. It makes sense not to waste it!

Just as with energy, the government is trying to encourage us all to stop wasting precious water.

Key terms

Space-zoning: a way of reducing conflict between different users of, e.g. a reservoir, by restricting them to different areas.

Transpiration: the process by which water absorbed by plants, usually through roots, is evaporated into the atmosphere from the plant surface, especially the leaves.

Activity

2 Map **F** shows the demand for water in England and Wales in 1990 and projections for 2021.

a In which area is there the greatest predicted percentage change in demand for water?

b In which area are planners predicting that population or industrial activity will decline?

Source: AQA 2001

xxx	1990 regional demand (Ml day⁻¹)
xxx	Baseline 2021 demand projected (Ml day⁻¹)
xx%	% change 1990-2021

F *Water demand in England and Wales*

Activity

3 Make a list of 10 simple ways of reducing water use in your home. Compare your list with a friend and select the best 10. Try to put them in order with the one that will save the most water as number one and so on.

Toilets are responsible for about 30 per cent of the water used in homes and this is an area where it is easy to cut water use:

- don't flush the toilet on every visit
- install a water displacement device (brick) to reduce the amount of water used per flush
- install a new dual flush toilet.

Other ideas you might have had include: repairing leaks; having showers instead of baths; replacing old washing machines and dishwashers with newer, energy- and water-saving models; only filling kettles with just enough water for your needs; and using bath water to flush the toilet.

Water companies are also trying to conserve water by replacing very old pipes and by encouraging people to fit water meters as these make people aware of how much water they use. When necessary, the companies are also able to impose hosepipe bans.

The 2007 floods

In July 2007, Gloucestershire experienced the worst floods on record. Underground sewers flowed on to the streets and into people's homes. The River Severn flooded the Mythe Water Treatment Works in Tewkesbury and left 150 000 people without clean water for drinking or cooking. The entire water supply system was contaminated. Water engineers worked day and night for two weeks firstly to drain the contaminated water from the plant and pipes and then decontaminate all the equipment at the plant. This was the first time ever that an entire water supply network had to be emptied and recharged.

G *The flooded Mythe Water Treatment Works*

How do water companies treat water to make it safe to drink?

The water held in reservoirs is sent to a water treatment plant before it is put into the pipes that eventually lead to taps in the home and elsewhere.

Water quality is tested at water treatment works, in the actual pipes and at consumers' taps. Scientists from water companies in England and Wales carry out nearly 3 million tests on our drinking water every year. Tests include those for nitrates, phosphates, ammonia, cloudiness, bacteria like *E. coli* (found in faeces), toxic metals like lead, pH and pesticides. Scientists also monitor the presence or absence of living organisms such as fish and certain insects, as these act as indicators of pollution. Over 99 per cent of samples pass the chemical tests – the water that comes out of your taps is some of the cleanest water in the world!

There are several stages in water treatment. In general, water drawn from aquifers is cleaner than that drawn from rivers and reservoirs and needs less treatment. Water from lowland rivers require the most treatment of all.

H   *Water treatment*

Process	Description
Screening	Grid removes large floating objects, e.g. branches and plastic bags
Clarification	Water allowed to become still and objects denser than the water sink to the bottom
	Chemicals are used to make finer particles in suspension clump together which can then be removed by settlement or by skimming them off the surface
Filtration	Sand or charcoal filter beds are used to remove any remaining particles along with colours, odours and pesticides
Disinfection	Chlorine or ozone is used to kill bacteria and some viruses

AQA *Examiner's tip*

Don't confuse the treatment of drinking water with sewage treatment!

Measuring water pollution

Scientists from the Environment Agency investigated whether a local dairy was polluting a shallow river by discharging hot water into it. They measured the water temperature upstream of the dairy, at the point where the dairy discharged into the river, and downstream of the dairy. At each site they measured the water temperature four times with a hand-held thermometer and once using a sophisticated electronic sensor. Table **I** shows their results.

At which site were the measurements using the hand-held thermometer:

- precise but not accurate
- accurate but not precise
- accurate and precise?

I

Site	Temperature from hand-held thermometer/ °C	Average temperature/ °C	Actual water temperature taken using electronic sensor/ °C
Upstream	7, 7, 8, 8	7.5	8
At the dairy	10, 7, 4, 9	7.5	8
Downstream	5, 5, 5, 6	5.3	8

How science works

Summary

Water supplies are obtained from aquifers, rivers and reservoirs.

Scientists monitor rainfall and water levels in rivers, reservoirs and aquifers and try to ensure supply matches demand.

Planners try to design and manage resources such as reservoirs so that combinations of different users can enjoy the resource.

Water is a precious resource. Nationally and individually, there are many things that can be done to help conserve the resource.

Water treatment ensures that the water that reaches homes is safe to drink.

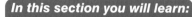

B2.3   What happens to waste water?

There are 20 million households in England alone. Every day each household flushes four gallons of sewage down the toilet. Where does it all go and how is waste water treated so that it is safe to put back in rivers and be used again?

■ Why is waste water treatment necessary?

Waste water is made up of all the water that goes down sinks and toilets plus the water which runs off the land into the drains.

Sewage consists of domestic and industrial liquid wastes, including urine and faecal material. It is 99.9 per cent water but contains dissolved organic and inorganic compounds, suspended solids, disease-causing organisms (**pathogens**) and the eggs of parasitic round worms, tape worms and flukes. It looks and smells unpleasant too!

Before the introduction of sewers (underground pipes that carry away sewage), people simply threw their urine and faeces (and everything else) onto the street or into open ditches that sloped away to the nearest river or into the sea. This created a major health hazard and a serious threat to the environment! It took a series of cholera epidemics (1830–1850), frequent fires and explosions caused by methane and the 'Big Stink' years (1858–1859), during which the low-flowing Thames failed to carry away sewage, to stimulate the government to adopt a national strategy for dealing with sewage.

Sewage contains organic matter – indigestible plant material, for example. If this enters water, bacteria will begin to decompose it. In so doing, they will use up most of the oxygen in the water. Most organisms that require oxygen (aerobes) will suffocate. Sewage also contains plant nutrients such as nitrates and phosphates. If these chemicals get into water bodies, they will cause eutrophication; algal blooms will develop. When the algae die, they too are decomposed by oxygen-consuming bacteria and the water will become de-oxygenated.

When we flush the toilet, sewage is carried away through a system of sewer pipes, often connected to the storm drains on roads, to sewage treatment plants. Water is a finite resource so we need to recycle it if possible.

In this section you will learn:

why we need to treat waste water

about the physical and biological processes involved in sewage treatment.

Key terms

Pathogen: an organism that causes disease.

Activity

If raw sewage enters a river, bacterial populations increase because the organic matter provides food for them. The bacteria use oxygen dissolved in the water to break down the organic matter. The amount of oxygen that the bacteria need to break down the organic matter is called the biochemical oxygen demand (BOD).

1   Which graph shows how oxygen levels (O_2) and BOD would change downstream of an accidental sewage leak into a river?

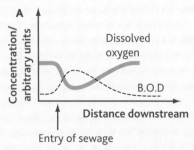

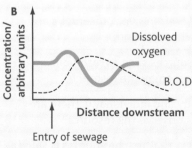

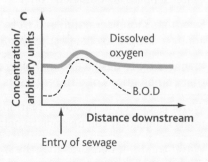

A

What processes are involved in sewage treatment?

Sewage treatment involves both physical and biological processes.

1 Sewage from households, mixed with water from street drains, enters a settlement tank through a screen. The screen separates out large solid objects such as grit and litter.

2 Most of the remaining organic matter is then allowed to settle to the bottom.

3 The remaining liquid is sprinkled through the air and trickles over stones. The stones have air spaces between them and provide a large surface area for millions of bacteria to feed on the proteins, carbohydrates and fats in the sewage. Trickling the sewage over the stones ensures that it mixes with oxygen allowing the micro-organisms to **aerobically** respire and break down the sewage. A pump adds extra oxygen into the sewage.

4 The sewage sludge that sinks to the bottom of the aeration tank is fed into an enclosed tank and is digested by **anaerobic** bacteria. Sometimes, this tank is warmed to around 35 °C, the optimum for bacterial respiration. The bacteria break down proteins in the sewage sludge and release methane gas which can be collected and burned to provide heating or even used to generate electricity.

5 The liquid is now free of pathogens and organic matter and is returned to a river or the sea.

6 The sludge is dried and either disposed of in landfill sites or, if free from heavy metals, used by farmers to increase the amount of organic matter in their soil.

Key terms

Aerobic: using oxygen.

Anaerobic: without oxygen.

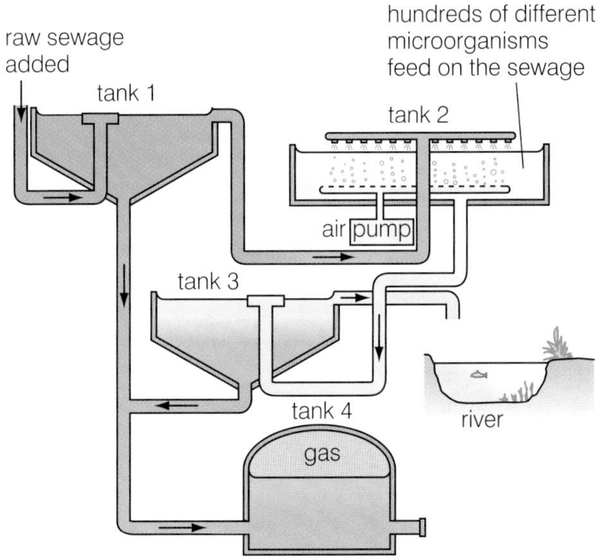

B *Sewage treatment*

Sitting higher tier

Finally, some sewage plants carry out 'nutrient stripping'. This involves chemically removing nitrates and phosphates from the liquid. This may be necessary to prevent eutrophication and algal blooms in coastal areas and where shellfish are caught.

Key terms

Sitting higher tier

Nutrient-stripping: the removal of nitrates and phosphates from treated effluent.

Waste water treatment engineer

'I work at Mogden waste water treatment plant. Mogden treats 450 million litres of Londoners' sewage every day. That's from about 1.8 million people!

We produce about 100 000 tonnes of sludge annually which is taken to the Perry Oaks Works, on the western edge of Heathrow Airport. The sludge is dried in evaporation ponds and turned into sludge cake for agricultural use.

Clean water is returned to the Thames.

My job involves monitoring the volume of intake. This is tricky because we receive sewage mixed with water from storm drains. In really wet periods, like much of this summer, our intake can dramatically increase. I also monitor the level of organic matter and suspended solids in the water that we return to the Thames. The quality of the water has to meet standards set by the Environment Agency. Again, this can be tricky. In dry summers, like in 1995, the volume of the Thames is much reduced. At times like this, we are returning daily twice the actual river's volume!'

C   *Mogden waste water treatment plant*

Activity

Diagram **D** shows a section through an aerobic digestion tank at a sewage treatment works.

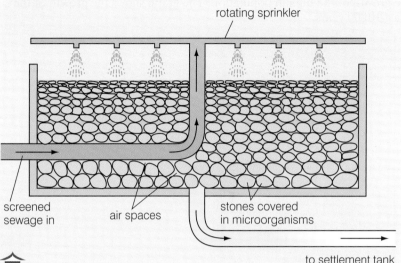

rotating sprinkler

screened sewage in

air spaces

stones covered in microorganisms

to settlement tank

D

2   **a**   What features, shown in the diagram, encourage aerobic respiration?

b   What happens if raw sewage enters a river?

AQA *Examiner's tip*

When answering this question, many candidates claim that the fish die because of toxins in the sewage or that the bacteria caused disease. Make sure that you refer to the organic matter in the sewage and that its breakdown by bacteria removes oxygen from the water.

Summary

Sewage treatment aims to remove bacteria and other pathogens and to produce an effluent that does not smell or look unpleasant.

Sewage treatment involves both physical and biological processes.

Physical processes remove large objects such as grit and twigs. Biological processes breakdown (decompose) the organic matter.

The final liquid is returned to the sea or to a river. The sludge is taken to a landfill site or used on farmers' fields.

Examination-style questions

1 Population scientists study the growth of the human population. The graph shows the growth of the human population over the past 10000 years.

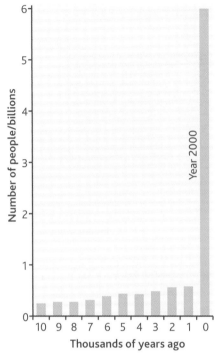

(a) Describe **one** way in which the change in human population shown in the graph differs from the population change of any other animal species. *(1 mark)*

(b) Suggest **three** reasons why human population growth has been able to increase in the way shown. *(3 marks)*

Sitting higher tier

2 **(a)** What is sustainable development? *(2 marks)*

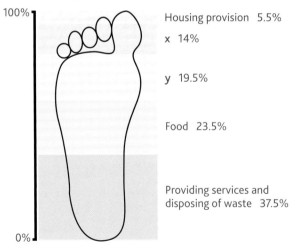

(b) The diagram shows some of the things that make up a person's ecological footprint.

   (i) Suggest what components of the ecological footprint could be represented by **x** and **y**.

   (ii) Explain why, in the past, as countries become more developed, they release more CO_2 and create a bigger ecological footprint. *(4 marks)*

3   Energy consultants carry out surveys and give advice on how to save energy. The diagram shows where energy is lost in a typical home.

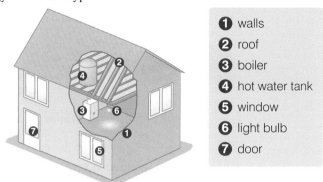

1 walls
2 roof
3 boiler
4 hot water tank
5 window
6 light bulb
7 door

List **three** ways in which energy loss from this home could be reduced. For each technique, explain why it would reduce energy loss.   (*6 marks*)

4   Copy and complete the following passage that describes some of the energy changes involved in wind power. You can use the list of words to help you.

Energy from the ………….. is absorbed by the Earth's surface. The surface of the Earth warms and re-radiates …………. energy. The energy that is re-radiated warms the air above it and causes it to ………….. . This creates air …………. that have …………. energy. This energy turns wind turbines that may be sited on land or at ………….. . The turbines drive generators that convert this energy into ………….. energy. However, not all the energy is turned into useful energy. Some is lost as………….. .

currents	rise
sea	electrical
Sun	kinetic
longwave	heat and noise

(*8 marks*)

5   The diagram shows the natural greenhouse effect.
     Which letter represents:
     (a) reflected radiation
     (b) longwave radiation
     (c) shortwave radiation?   (*3 marks*)

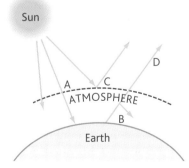

Sitting higher tier

6   In many parts of the world, bee populations are falling. Scientists are not sure why but believe it may be due to a combination of disease, parasites, pollution and climate change.

Suggest why humans should try to conserve bees in order to maintain world food supplies.

(2 marks)

7   Conservationists are worried that the giant panda is threatened with extinction.

Giant pandas live only in very small, widely scattered populations in China and feed only on bamboo. China's population is growing and the country is developing extremely rapidly. Recently, attempts have been made to start a captive breeding programme.

(a) Suggest **three** reasons why the giant panda is threatened with extinction.   *(3 marks)*

(b) Suggest how a captive breeding programme could help to save the pandas and maintain biodiversity.   *(4 marks)*

8   Scientists employed by Defra work closely with farmers to prevent pollution of drinking water supplies by agricultural activities.

The diagram shows some of the operations on a typical farm that grows crops and raises livestock.

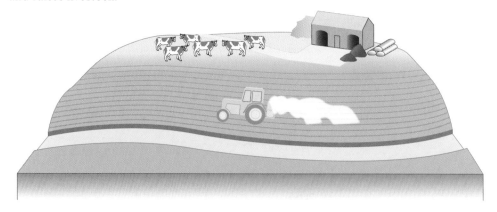

(a) Describe how agricultural activities can cause water pollution.   *(6 marks)*

(b) Explain how this pollution can be avoided or reduced.   *(4 marks)*

Glossary

A

Abstraction: removing water from a source so that it can be used elsewhere.

Accuracy: how close your measurements are to the true value. Taking repeat measurements increases accuracy.

Aerobic: using oxygen.

Anaerobic: without oxygen.

Anomalies: measurements or results that are clearly out of line.

Aquifer: a porous, permeable underground rock such as chalk or sandstone that contains water in millions of pores.

Artificial fertilisers: nitrates, phosphates and potassium that are added to the soil to increase crop growth.

B

Biodiversity: the number and variety of species within a region.

Biofuels: renewable energy resources such as energy crops, wood wastes, biogas and biodiesel.

Birth rate: the ratio of live births in an area to the population of that area, usually expressed as 'per thousand (people) per year'.

Botanic garden: a research institute where rare or important plant species are grown in order to protect the species from extinction.

By-catch: unwanted species (for example fish, turtles, dolphins) caught in fishing nets. The organisms are then thrown back, dead, into the sea.

C

Captive breeding: the breeding of species in captivity, usually zoos, with the aim of reintroducing the animals back to their original habitat once it is safe to do so.

Carbon capture and storage: removal of CO_2 from waste gases at power stations and then storing it in old oil and gas fields or in old mines.

Carbon footprint: the environmental impact of the total amount of carbon dioxide, and other greenhouse gases, emitted over the full life cycle of the use of a product, service or event by individuals, specific human activities or areas.

Carbon licence: bought by companies who pay to emit a certain amount of carbon dioxide.

Carbon neutral: an energy source, e.g. sugar beet, that, when burned, releases no net CO_2. The amount of CO_2 released equals that which was absorbed by the plant in photosynthesis.

Carbon offsetting: paying for trees to be planted to absorb CO_2 to make up for that which was released by a person's activity, e.g. flying abroad.

Carbon tax: a tax that has to be paid by industry according to how much CO_2 they emit. It aims to encourage industry to release less CO_2.

Climate refugees: people who are forced to flee their regions or countries because of flooding or other environmental problems caused by climate change.

Combustion: burning.

Controlled environment: an environment in which the factors that affect crop growth, e.g. light, temperature, ventilation, are carefully controlled to maximise growth.

Coastal erosion: the destruction of the coastline by sea surges, storms and higher sea levels caused by climate change.

Coppicing: a traditional form of woodland management that involves cutting trees down to a stump in order to encourage the growth of several new shoots.

D

Death rate: the ratio of deaths in an area to the population of that area, usually expressed as 'per thousand (people) per year'.

Deforestation: the felling of forests.

Dependent variable: the variable that you are measuring each time you change the independent variable.

E

Ecological footprint: the amount of the Earth's resources of an area that a person or group consumes to support their lifestyle

Energy conservation: the practice of decreasing the amount of energy used in the home. This is often by reducing heat loss and using more efficient appliances.

Energy consultant: a person whose job involves checking the amount of energy used in homes, businesses and public services and giving advice on how to save energy.

Energy density: the amount of energy contained in a unit of an energy source, e.g. 1 g of plutonium contains a lot more energy than 1 g of coal.

Erosion: the loss of soil as it is washed and blown away.

European Community Energy Label: a label showing how energy-efficient an electrical device is. These labels must appear on most household electrical items sold in the EU. They are intended to help buyers choose the most efficient devices.

Eutrophication: the artificial enrichment of water with too many inorganic nutrients, such as nitrates and phosphates.

Extinct: a species for which there has been no confirmed sighting for 50 years.

F

Fair test: one in which the only thing affecting the dependent variable is the independent variable that you are changing or selecting.

Food miles: the distance food travels through the complete production process until it reaches the consumer.

Fossil fuels: these are fuels formed from the remains of dead plants and animals. The three main fossil fuels are coal, oil and natural gas. They were formed millions of years ago.

G

Genetically modified organism: an organism that has had its genetic material altered in a way that does not occur naturally by mating.

Geothermal energy: heat from the radioactive decay of elements within the Earth.

H

Habitat: the natural conditions in which an organism, animal or plant lives.

Hydrologist: a water scientist.

Hypothesis: an idea that might explain the relationship under investigation.

I

Independent variable: the variable that you, as investigator, change or select.

Indicator species: a common and easily identified species, e.g. an invertebrate whose presence or absense implies certain pollution levels.

Intensification: the use of many inputs (fertiliser, pesticide, mechanisation) in order to increase outputs (food).

Intermittency: the way in which energy from some sources, e.g. wind, starts and stops according to how strongly the wind blows.

L

Land degradation: the decrease in the capacity of the land to produce (food) caused by human activity and natural processes, e.g. soil erosion.

LEDC: Less Economically Developed Country. A country in which people are relatively poor and have a low per capita (per person) income. Birth rates and death rates are usually high. There is usually little industrialisation. Examples include Botswana and Vietnam.

Longwave radiation: this is the radiation which is re-radiated from the Earth's surface. It is mainly infrared radiation.

M

MEDC: More Economically Developed Country. A country in which people are relatively wealthy. Per capita income is relatively high. Birth and death rates are much lower than in LEDCs. MEDCs are usually industrialised. Examples include the UK and USA.

Meter: in UK English, a meter is a device used to measure something, e.g. an electricity meter; the unit of distance is a metre.

Montreal Protocol: an agreement by many countries to phase out production of substances, such as CFCs, that deplete the ozone layer.

N

Nuclear fission: the splitting of atoms to release vast amounts of energy.

Nuclear fusion: the process that occurs in the Sun, when extremely high temperatures cause atoms to join together, releasing vast amounts of energy.

Nutrient-stripping: the removal of nitrates and phosphates from treated effluent.

O

Overfishing: more fish are caught than are replaced by reproduction. It is biologically and economically unsustainable.

P

Pathogen: an organism that causes disease.

Pay-back time: the amount of time it takes for an energy-saving measure to pay for itself through savings on energy costs.

Permeability: the rate at which water can move through the pores in a rock.

Pest: a destructive animal which attacks crops and livestock.

Pesticides: chemicals designed to kill organisms that feed on or cause disease in crops, in order to reduce yield losses.

Photosynthesis: the process by which plants (and some micro-organisms) make food using carbon dioxide, water and light energy.

Pollution: undesirable change in the physical, chemical or biological characteristics of land, air and water which can harm the lives of humans and other organisms.

Population growth rate: a measure of population change, usually the natural rate of increase of the population. Birth rate ± death rate (per year).

Porosity: the amount of pore space in a rock.

Precision: how closely grouped your repeat measurements are.

Predator: an animal that hunts others for food.

Predictability: what is the certainty that an energy source will deliver the right amount of energy when it is needed, e.g. tidal power is predictable.

Q

Quota: the maximum weight of fish of a particular species that can be caught in a year.

R

Reliable: data is reliable if someone else can repeat what you did and get the same results.

Reservoir: an artificial lake for collecting and storing water.

Respiration: the process by which organisms break down their food to release energy. Respiration can be aerobic (using oxygen) or anaerobic (happening without oxygen).

Ruminants: livestock such as cattle, goats, sheep and buffalo that release methane as they digest grass.

S

Salinisation: the build-up of salts in soils that is toxic to plant roots.

Seed bank: a repository of plant seeds that have been dried or frozen and stored. If needed, the seeds can be germinated years later and used to reintroduce the plant to wherever it is required.

Selective breeding: the selection by humans of individuals to breed together, based upon their useful characteristics.

Shortwave radiation: the radiation which comes from the Sun and warms the Earth's surface. This radiation is mainly visible light.

Soil degradation: the breakdown and loss of fertility of soil.

Space-zoning: a way of reducing conflict between different users of, e.g. a reservoir, by restricting them to different areas.

Stud book: an international register, updated every 3 years, which lists all captive individuals of a species which is under threat.

Sustainable: capable of being carried on forever which means living within environmental limits.

Sustainable development: development which meets present needs without compromising the ability of future generations to achieve their needs and aspirations.

T

Total Allowable Catch (TAC): the total amount of fish, in tonnes, that can be caught from a particular stock by a vessel over a year.

Thermal Imaging Survey: a survey using a camera which detects infrared radiation rather than visible light. Energy consultants use these cameras to find out where most heat is being lost from buildings.

Total fertility rate: the average number of children each woman has over her lifetime.

Transpiration: the process by which water absorbed by plants, usually through roots, is evaporated into the atmosphere from the plant surface, especially the leaves.

U

Unsustainable: a resource is being used unsustainably if it is being used faster than it can be formed again (in other words if it is a non-renewable resource) or if using the resource produces harmful waste or pollution.

V

Validity: the extent to which your results answer the question asked. Valid data has to be reliable and relevant.

Index

Acknowledgements

The authors and publisher are grateful to the following for permission to reproduce photographs and other copyright material in this book.

Photo research by Kay Altwegg.

Alamy: A & J Visage B1.1A; Arco Images GmbH B1.2G; Arctic Images A3.2B; Ashley Cooper B2.2G; Clynt Garnham Energy A2.1Bb; David J. Green B1.2I; Graeme Peacock B2.2D; Graham Harrison A2.1Ba; imagebroker A2.2A; ipk B1.2T; Jason Bye A3.4F; Jenny Matthews A1.1F; John Cancalosi B1.2Z; Juniors Bildarchiv B1.2V; Mediablitzimages (UK) Limited A1.3Ka; Paul Glendell B1.2AA; Pick and Mix Images A1.3Ke; Realimage A2.1C; Steven May A1.4F; The Photolibrary Wales B2.2C; **AP Photo:** Rajesh Kumar Singh A3.4I; **BiogenGreenfinch:** A1.2A; **Corbis:** Jonathan Blair B1.3A; **David Wootton (rspb-images.com):** B1.2AE; **Dorling Kindersley:** B1.2H; **Energy Saving Trust:** A2.2C; **Environment Agency:** B1.2Qi; **Flickr:** Drewhound B1.2AB; **FLPA:** David Hosking B1.2Y; Frans Lanting B1.1O; Ian Rose B1.2R; Imagebroker/Jorn Friederich B1.1E; Mike J Thomas B1.1I; Minden Pictures/Pete Oxford B1.1P; Minden Pictures/Thomas Marent B1.1H; Nigel Cattlin A1.3G; Phil McLean B1.1K; R. Dirscherl B1.3B; **Fotolia:** Bohanka A1; Desertdiver B1; Michael Keighery A2.1Ad; Rick Thornton A3.3H; **Golden Rice Humanitarian Board www.goldenrice.org:** A1.3B; **Konrad Steffen and Russell Huff, CIRES, University of Colorado at Boulder** A3.3D; **iStockphoto:** Adrian Matthiassen A2.4Fi; Al Fernandes HSW.C; Andy Gehrig B1.2U; Anneke Schram B1.2A; arlindo71 Q6; Brett Hillyard A2.4Fiv; Cathy Britcliffe A1.3Kc; Chris Crafter A1.4C; Dale Klonin Q7; Dirk Freder B1.1D; Dirk Richter A1.3Jiii; Frank van Haalen B1.3E; globestock A2.4Fiii; Grant Davenport A1.3Jii; Grant Dougall A2.4H; Howard Sandler B1.2P; Jan Will A3; Jonathan Parry B1.1L; Leif Norman A2.4Fv; Melodie Sheppard A1.1J; Merijn van der Vliet A1.3Ji; Morgan Lane Photography A2.2B; Olga Utlyakova A2.1Aa; Patrick Laverdant A1.3Jiv; Ralph125 A3.4D; Rhoberazzi A2.4Fvii; Sabrina Dei Nobili A2.2G; Sally Wallis A1.3H; Sami Suni A1.3E; Sascha Burkard B1.2AG; Skip Odonnell A2.1Ab; Stephanie Howard A1.3Kb; Steve Stone B1.2E; Svetlana Tebenkova A2; William R. Minten A1.3Kd; Yiannos Ioannou A2.1Ac; **Kevin Byrne:** B1.2AC; B1.2AD; B1.2AF; **Mirrorpix:** B2.2B; **Natural England:** B1.2Qii; **NASA:** Goddard Space Flight Center Scientific Visualization Studio The Blue Marble data is courtesy of Reto Stockli (NASA/GSFC) A3.3E; **Press Association Images:** PRESSENS B1.3F; **RSPB:** B1.2Qiii; **Science Photo Library:** Adrian Bicker A1.4I; Bjorn Svensson A2.4Fii; Graeme Ewens A3.3C; Martin Bond A2.4Fvi; Ria Novosti A2.4E; Ted Kinsman A2.2F; **Thames Water:** B2, B2.3C; **WWF:** B1.2Qiv.

p79, p81, p116, p121 Crown copyright material is reproduced with the permission of the Controller of HMSO and the Queen's Printer for Scotland.

p17 © 2001 Population Reference Bureau, www.prb.org.

Every effort has been made to trace and contact all copyright holders and we apologise if any have been overlooked. The publisher will be pleased to make the necessary arrangements at the first opportunity.